MORE SIMPLE SONGS

ISBN 978-1-4950-6913-0

HAL•LEONARD® CORPORATION

7777 W. BLUEMOUND RD. P.O. BOX 13819 MILWAUKEE, WI 53213

T0066467

Visit Hal Leonard Online at
www.halleonard.com

All Right Now

Words and Music by Andy Fraser and Paul Rodgers

2

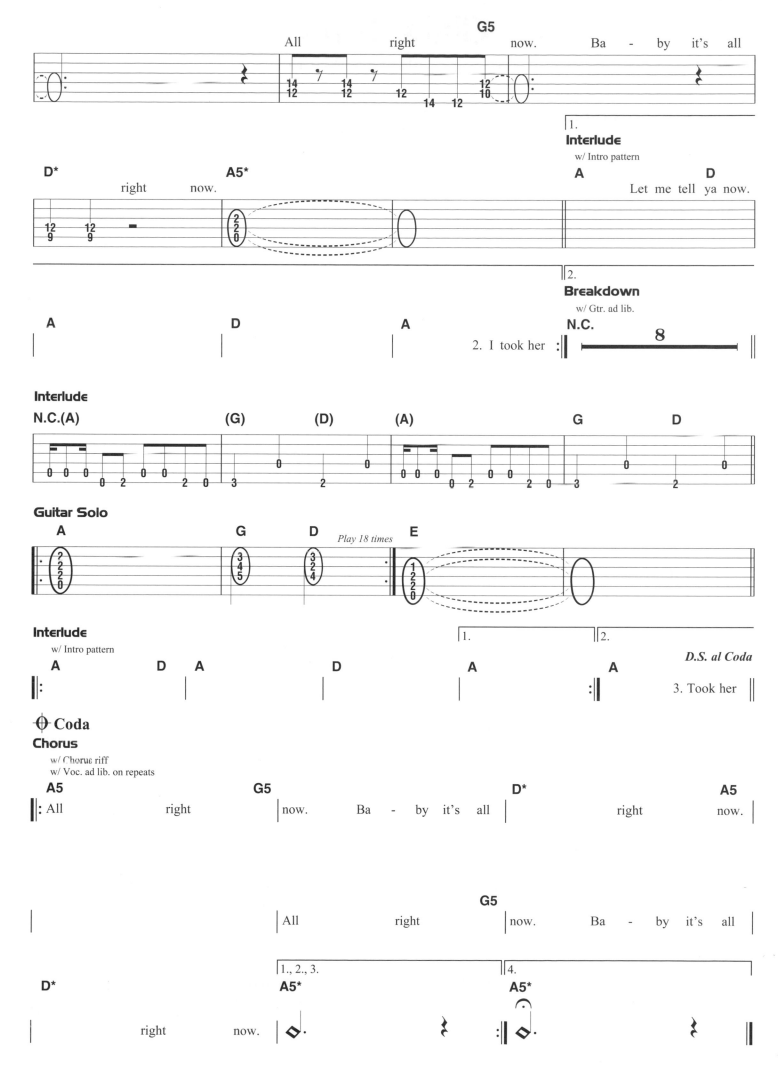

Billie Jean

Words and Music by Michael Jackson

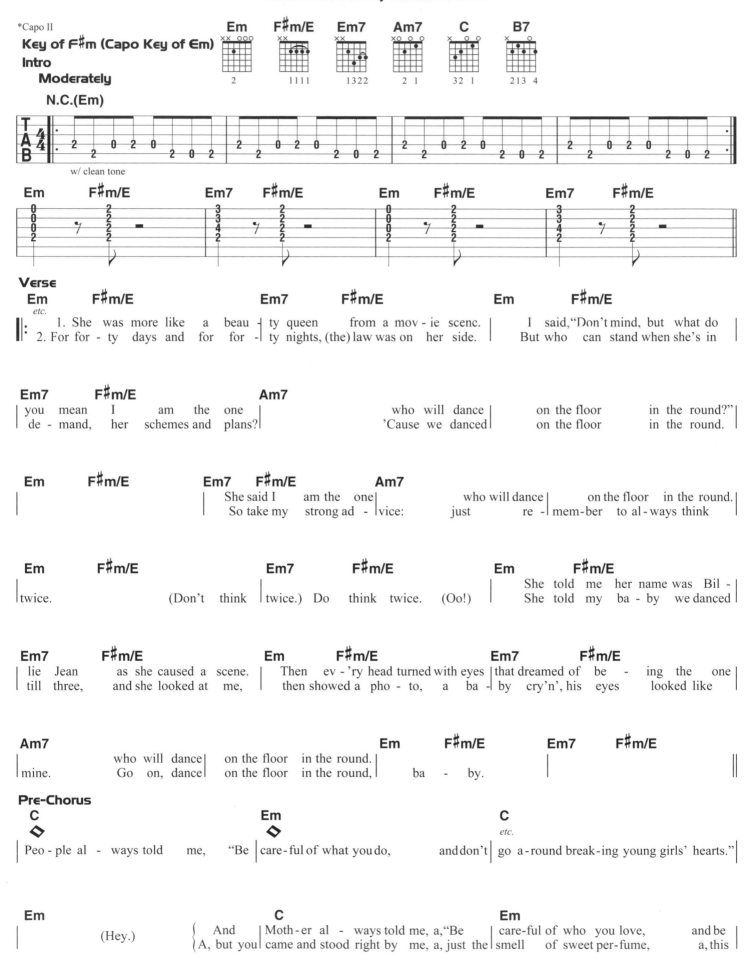

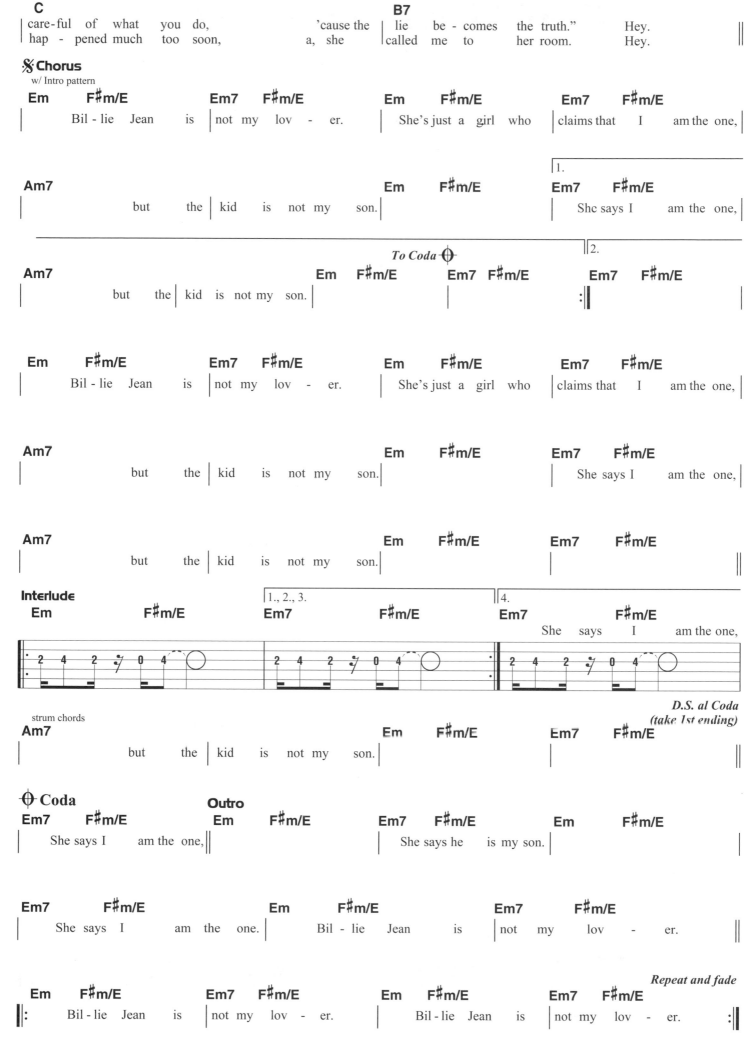

Born Under a Bad Sign

Words and Music by Booker T. Jones and William Bell

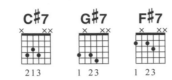

Key of C#

Intro

Moderately slow

Chorus

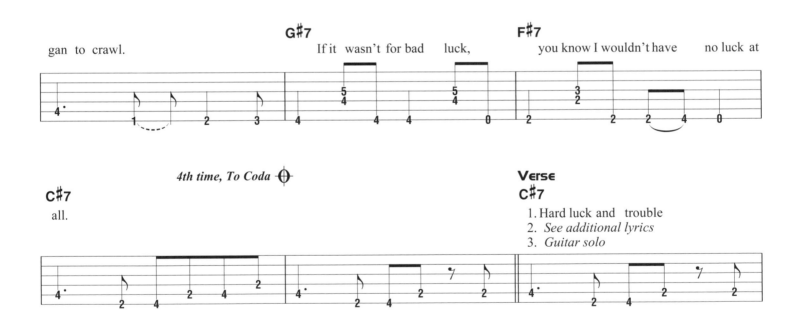

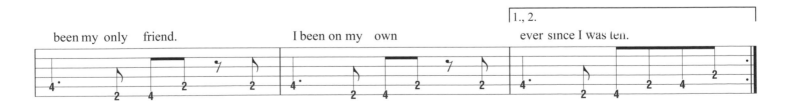

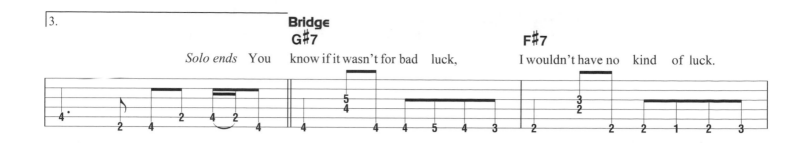

Additional Lyrics

2. I can't read, I didn't learn how to write.
   My whole life has been one big fight.

California Dreamin'

Words and Music by John Phillips and Michelle Phillips

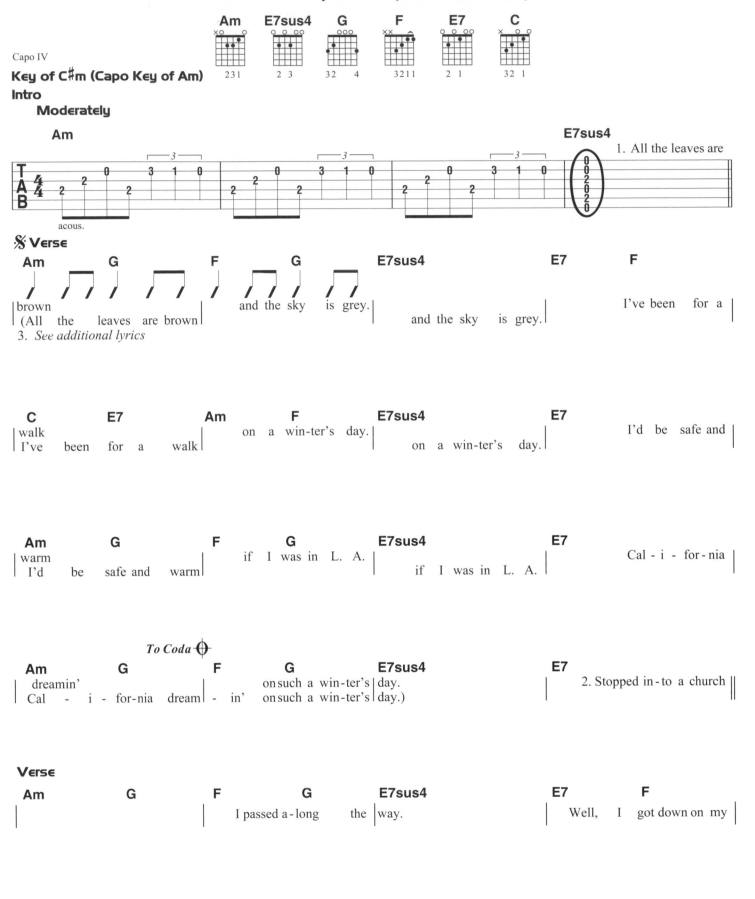

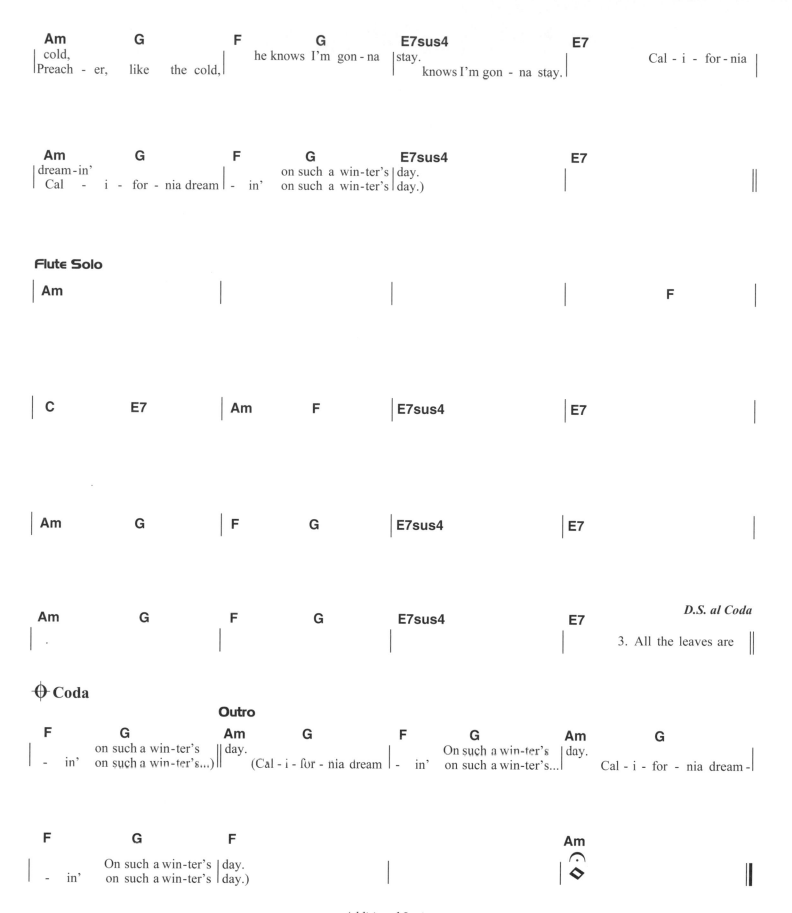

Am	G	F	G	E7sus4		E7	
cold,			he knows I'm gon - na	stay.			Cal - i - for - nia
Preach - er, like the cold,				knows I'm gon - na stay.			

Am	G	F	G	E7sus4		E7	
dream - in'			on such a win - ter's	day.			
Cal - i - for - nia dream		- in'	on such a win - ter's	day.)			

Flute Solo

Am					F	

C	E7	Am	F	E7sus4	E7	

Am	G	F	G	E7sus4	E7	

D.S. al Coda

Am	G	F	G	E7sus4	E7	
.						3. All the leaves are

Coda

Outro

F	G	Am	G	F	G	Am	G
- in'	on such a win - ter's	day.			On such a win - ter's	day.	
	on such a win - ter's...)	(Cal - i - for - nia dream	- in'	on such a win - ter's...		Cal - i - for - nia dream -

F	G	F		Am
- in'	On such a win - ter's	day.		
	on such a win - ter's	day.)		

Additional Lyrics

3. All the leaves are brown (All the leaves are brown)
And the sky is grey. (and the sky is grey.)
I've been for a walk (I've been for a walk)
On a winter's day. (on a winter's day.)
If I didn't tell her, (If I didn't tell her,)
I could leave today. (I could leave today.)
California dreamin' (California dreamin')
On such a winter's day. (on such a winter's...)

Can't Help Falling in Love

from the Paramount Picture BLUE HAWAII

Words and Music by George David Weiss, Hugo Peretti and Luigi Creatore

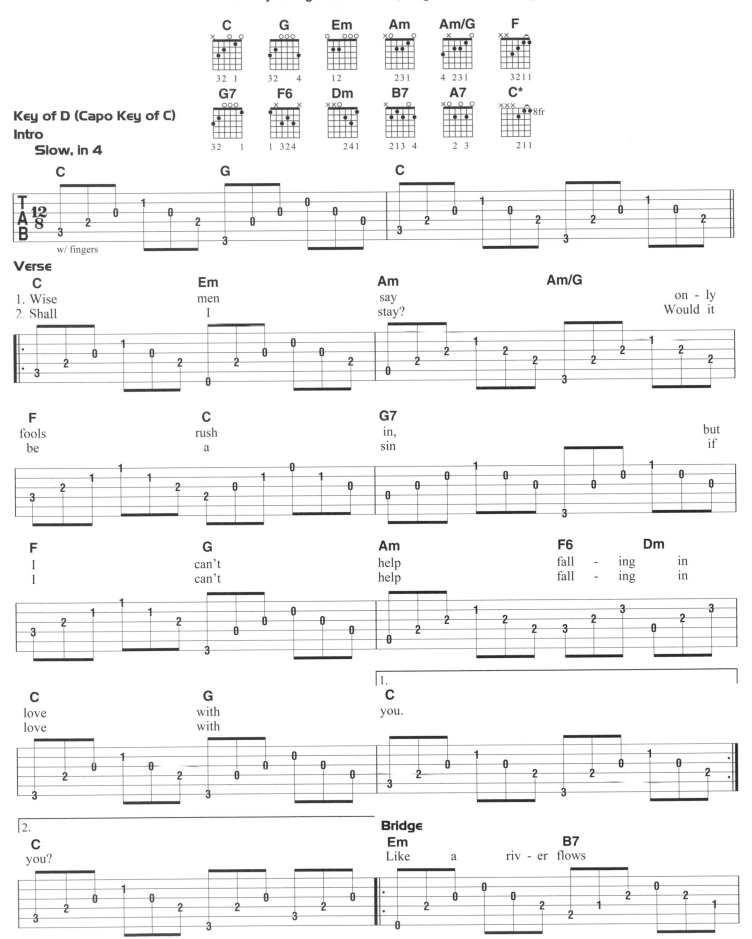

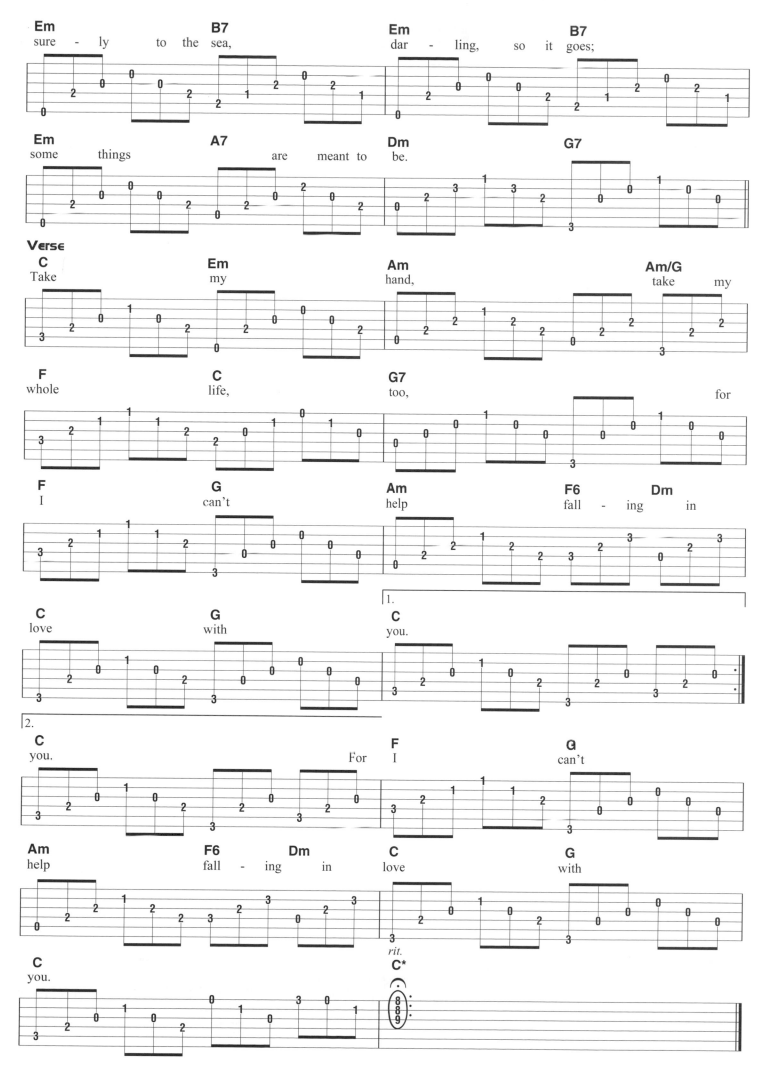

Carry On

Words and Music by Stephen Stills

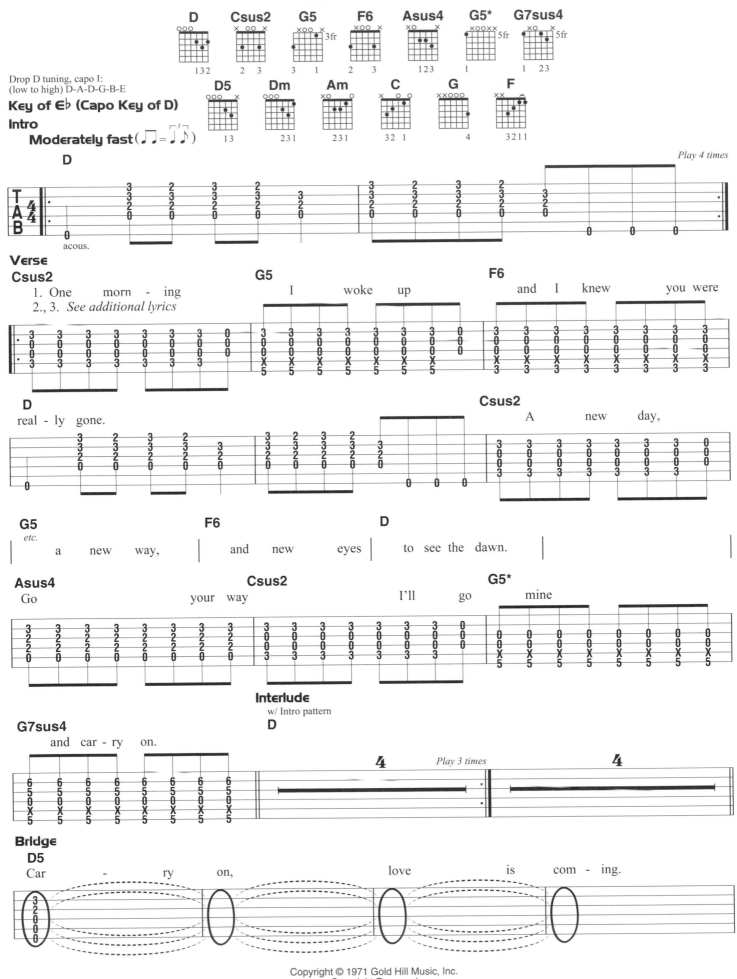

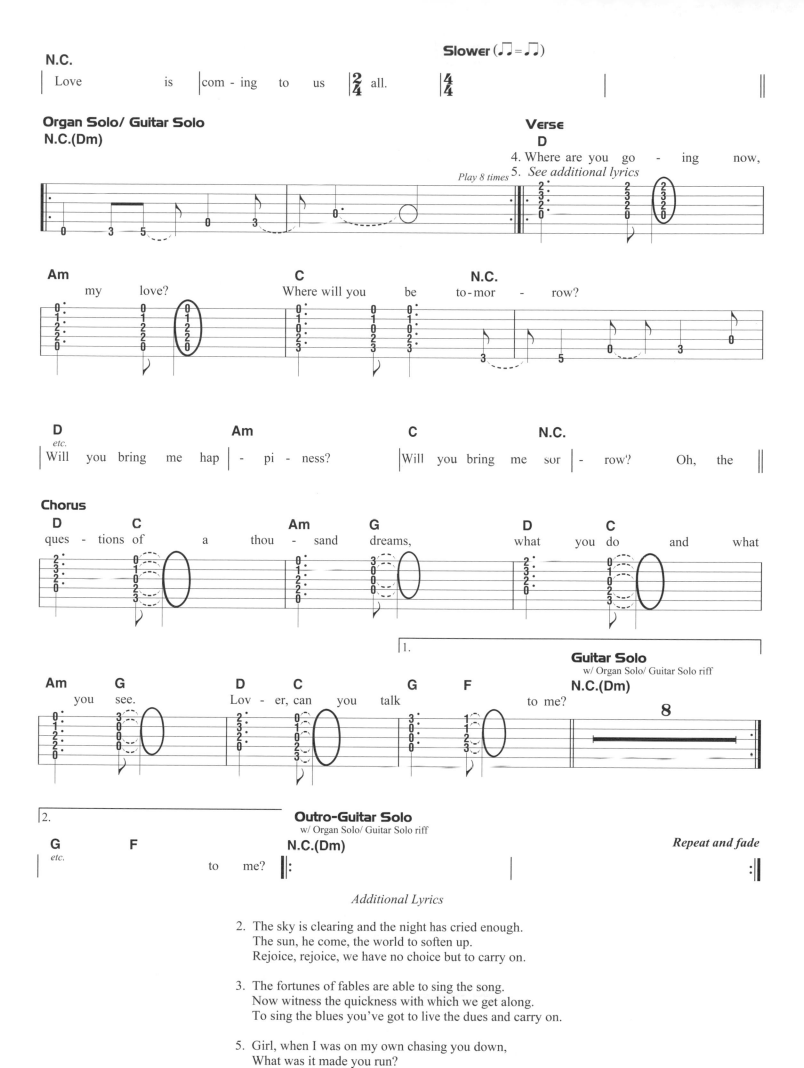

Come As You Are

Words and Music by Kurt Cobain

Tune down 1 step:
(low to high) D-G-C-F-A-D

Key of F#m

Intro

Moderately

N.C.

Play 4 times

w/ clean tone & chorus

§ Verse

N.C.
etc.

1. Come   as   you   are,   as   you   were,   as   I   want   you   to   be;
3. *Guitar Solo*

as   a   friend,   as   a   friend,   as   an   old

N.C.

en - e - my.   2. Come   Take   your   time,   hur - ry   up,
doused   in   mud,   soaked   in   bleach,

the   choice   is   yours,   don't   be   late.   Take   a   rest
as   I   want   you   to   be;   as   a   trend,

as   a   friend,   as   an   old   mem - o - ry,
as   a   friend,   as   an   old   mem - o - ry,
Guitar Solo ends   Mem - o - ry,

Pre-Chorus

F#sus4   A   F#sus4

ah,   mem - o - ry,   *etc.*   ah,

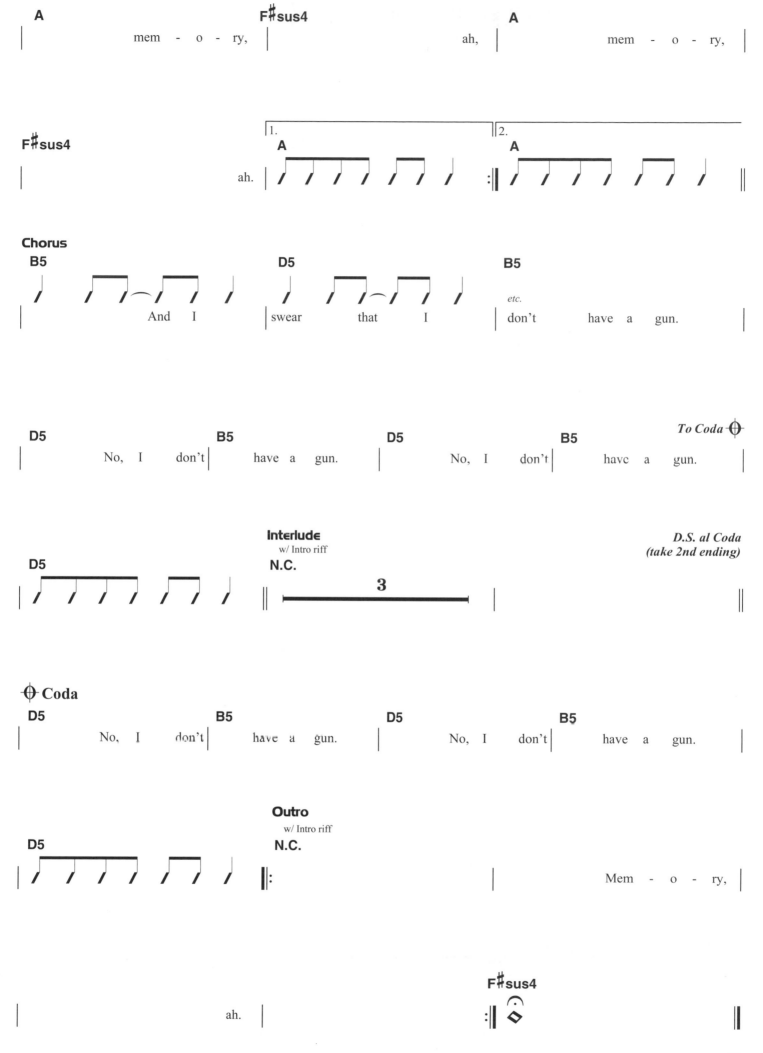

Cross Road Blues

(Crossroads)

Words and Music by Robert Johnson

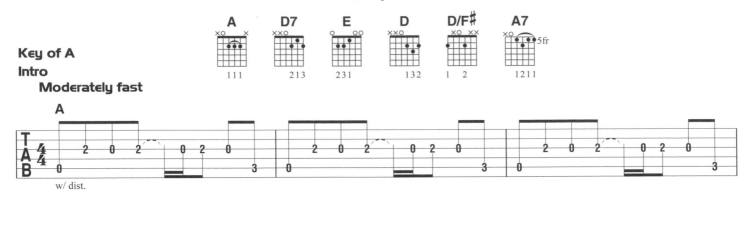

Key of A

Intro

Moderately fast

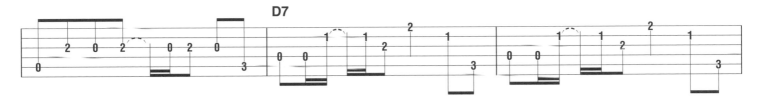

w/ dist.

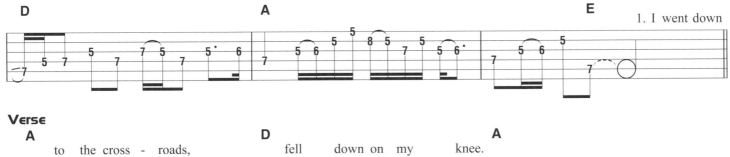

1. I went down

Verse

to the cross - roads,   fell down on my knee.

2. - 5. *See additional lyrics*

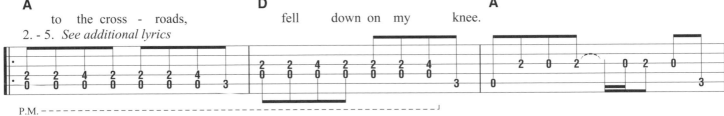

P.M.

Down to the cross - roads,   fell down on my knee.

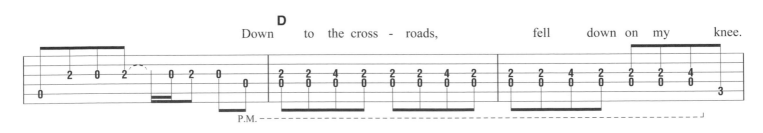

P.M.

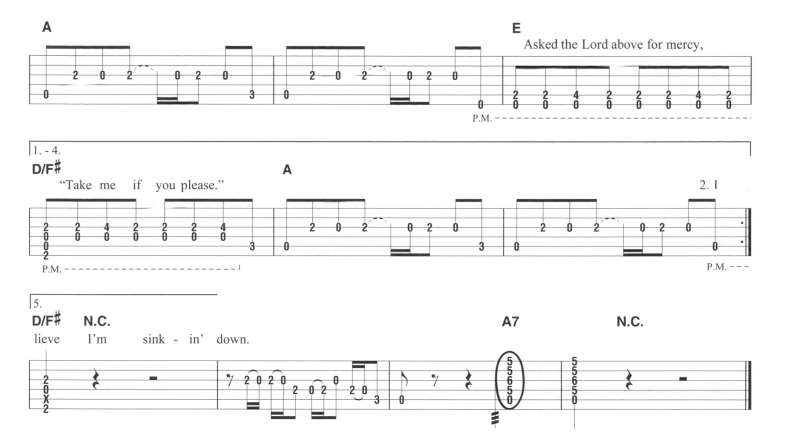

Additional Lyrics

2. I went down to the crossroad, tried to flag a ride.
   Down to the crossroad, tried to flag a ride.
   Nobody seemed to know me, ev'rybody passed by.

3. Well, I'm goin' down to Rosedale, take my rider by my side.
   Goin' down to Rosedale, take my rider by my side.
   We can still barrelhouse, baby, on the riverside.

4. Goin' down to Rosedale, take my rider by my side.
   Goin' down to Rosedale, take my rider by my side.
   We can still barrelhouse, baby, on the riverside.

5. You can run, you can run, tell my friend, boy, Willie Brown.
   Run you can run, tell my friend boy, Willie Brown.
   And I'm standin' at the crossroad, believe I'm sinkin' down.

Don't Let Me Be Lonely Tonight

Words and Music by James Taylor

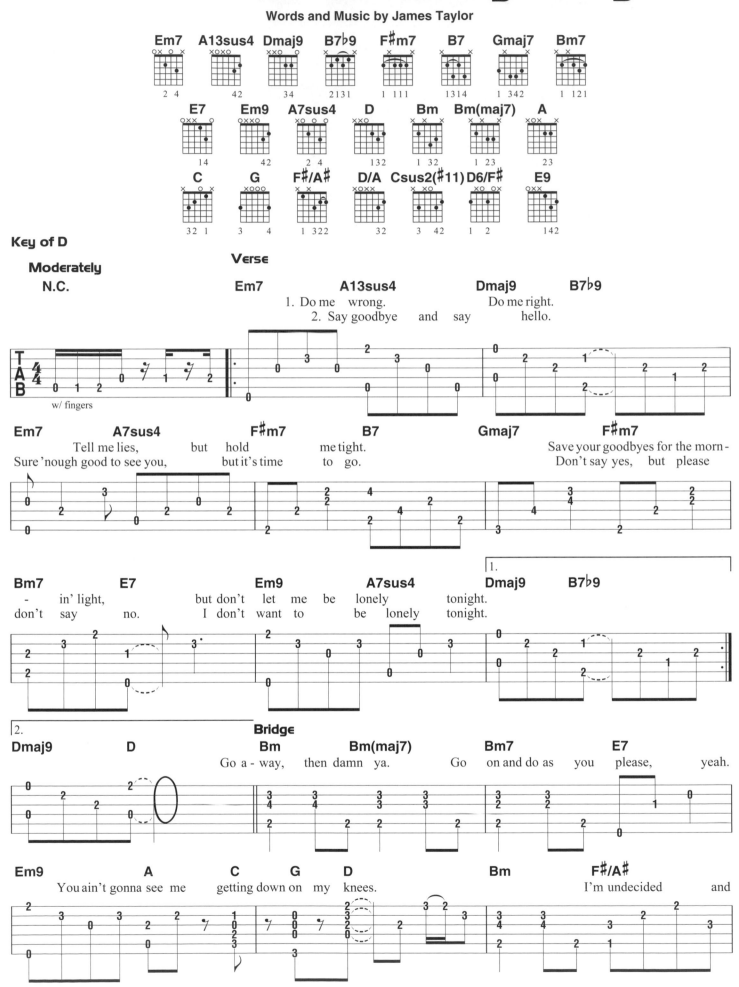

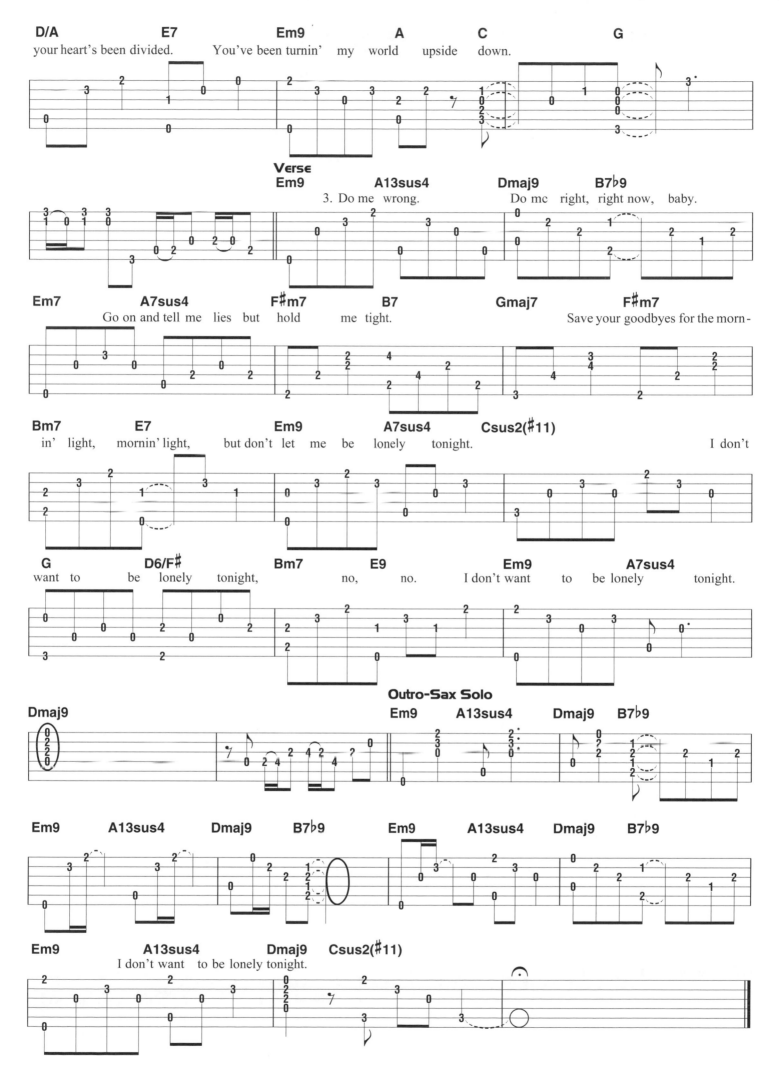

Europa

(Earth's Cry Heaven's Smile)

Words and Music by Carlos Santana and Tom Coster

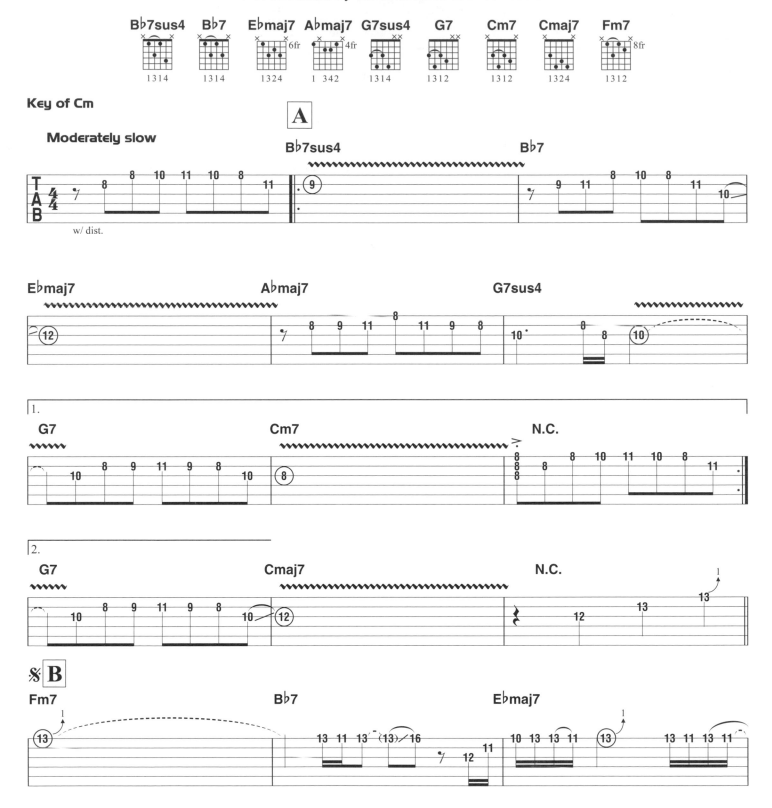

Key of Cm

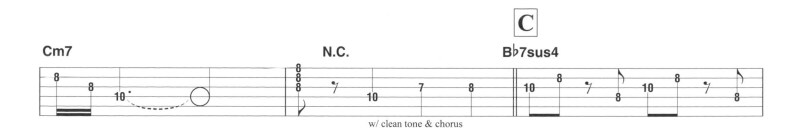

w/ clean tone & chorus

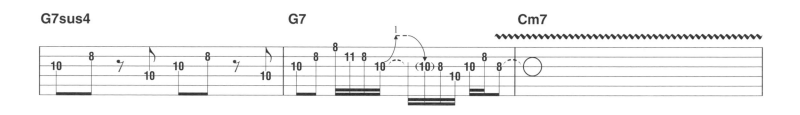

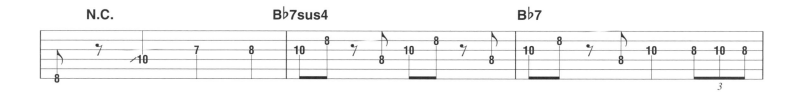

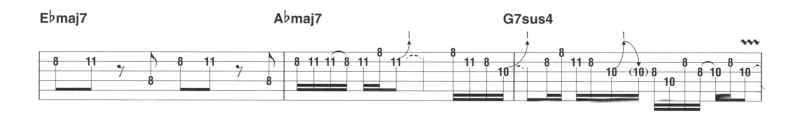

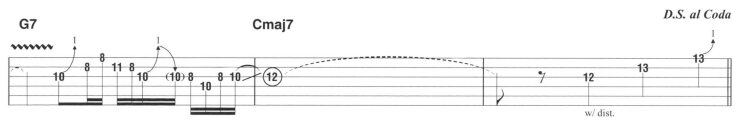

w/ dist.

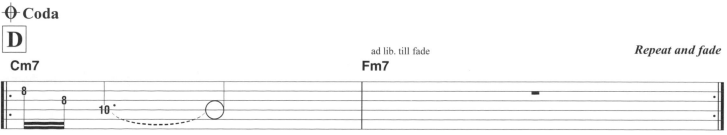

Friend of the Devil

Words by Robert Hunter
Music by Jerry Garcia and John Dawson

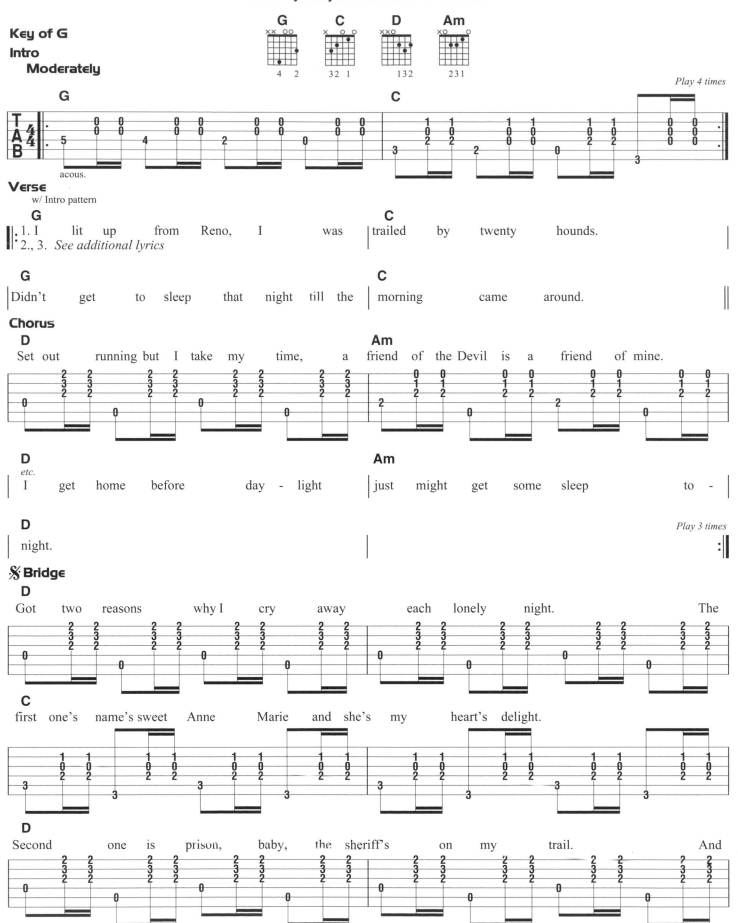

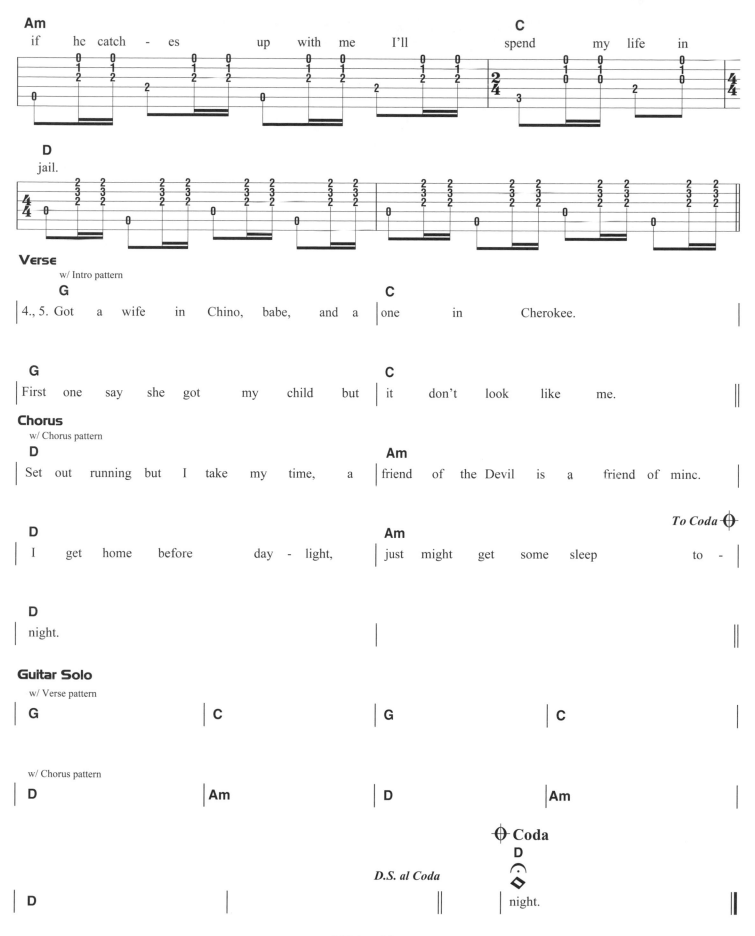

Verse
w/ Intro pattern

G   **C**
4., 5. Got a wife in Chino, babe, and a | one in Cherokee.

G   **C**
First one say she got my child but | it don't look like me.

Chorus
w/ Chorus pattern

D   **Am**
Set out running but I take my time, a | friend of the Devil is a friend of mine.

D   **Am**   *To Coda* ⊕
I get home before day - light, | just might get some sleep to -

D
night.

Guitar Solo
w/ Verse pattern

G | **C** | **G** | **C** |

w/ Chorus pattern

D | **Am** | **D** | **Am** |

                                  ⊕ **Coda**
                                  D
                        D.S. al Coda
D | ‖ | night.   ‖

Additional Lyrics

2. Ran into the Devil, babe, he loaned me twenty bills.
   Spent that night in Utah, in a cave up in the hills.

3. I ran down to the levee, but the Devil caught me there.
   Took my twenty dollar bill and he vanished in the air.

Hey, Soul Sister

Words and Music by Pat Monahan, Espen Lind and Amund Bjorklund

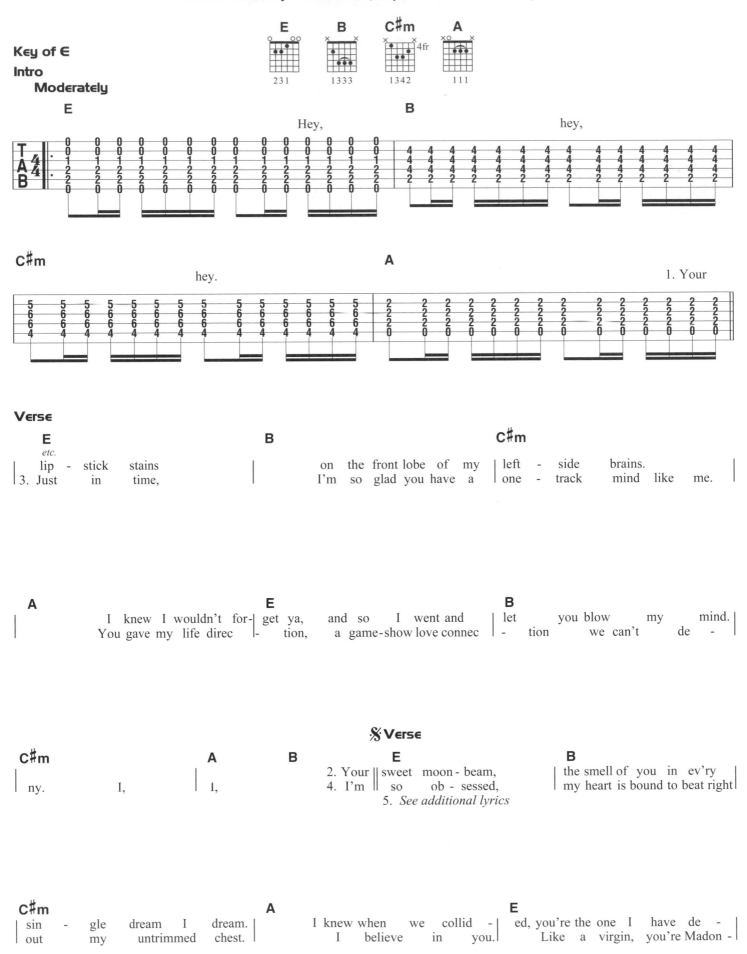

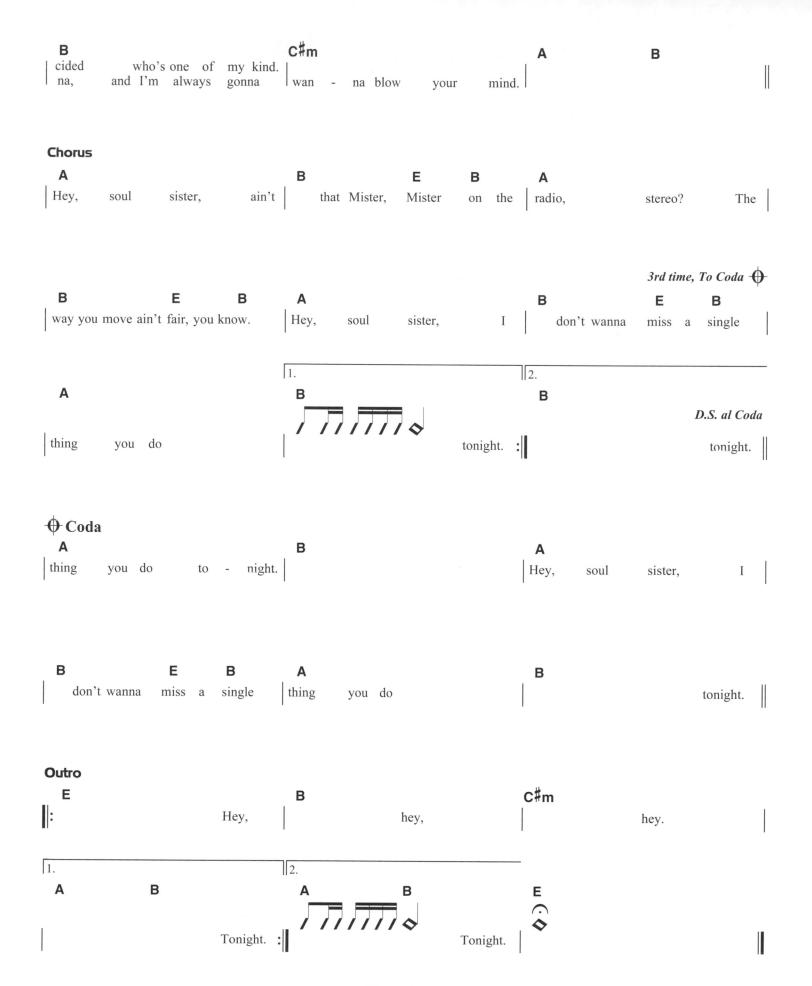

Hey There Delilah

Words and Music by Tom Higgenson

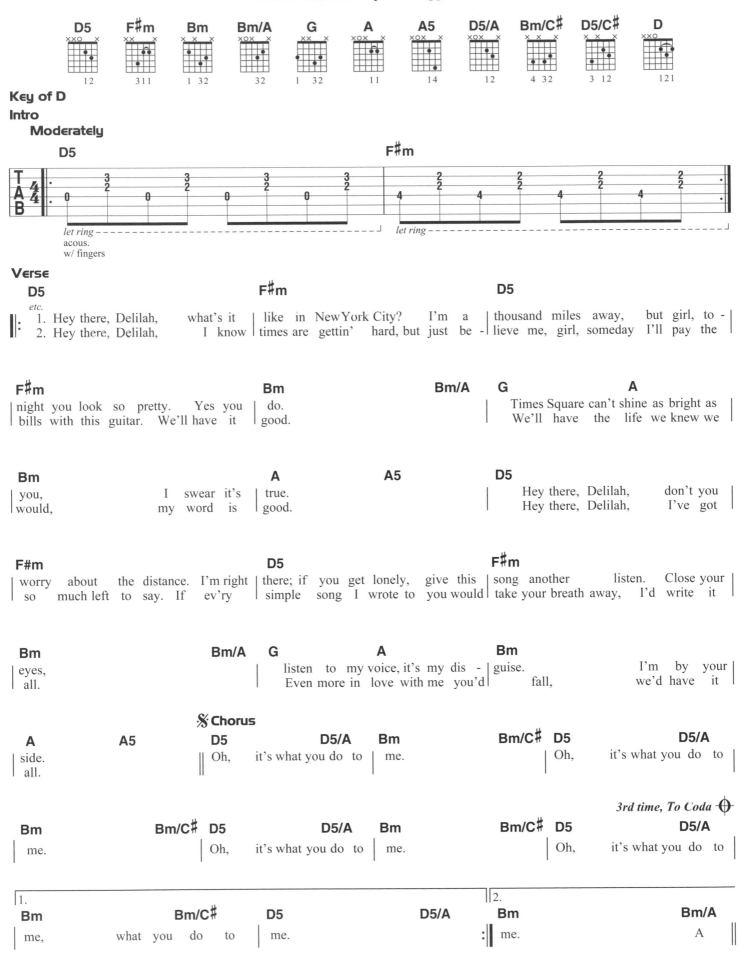

Key of D

Intro

Moderately

Verse

etc.

1. Hey there, Delilah,   what's it | like in New York City?   I'm a | thousand miles away,   but girl, to -

2. Hey there, Delilah,   I know | times are gettin' hard, but just be - | lieve me, girl, someday I'll pay the

night you look so pretty. Yes you | do. | Times Square can't shine as bright as

bills with this guitar. We'll have it | good. | We'll have the life we knew we

you,   I swear it's | true. | Hey there, Delilah,   don't you

would,   my word is | good. | Hey there, Delilah,   I've got

worry about the distance. I'm right | there; if you get lonely, give this | song another   listen. Close your

so much left to say. If ev'ry | simple song I wrote to you would | take your breath away, I'd write it

eyes, | listen to my voice, it's my dis - | guise.   I'm by your

all. | Even more in love with me you'd | fall,   we'd have it

Chorus

side. | Oh, it's what you do to | me. | Oh, it's what you do to

all. |

me. | Oh, it's what you do to | me. | Oh, it's what you do to

3rd time, To Coda

1.

me, what you do to | me. |

2.

me. | A

Bridge

| G | | A | D5 | D5/A |

thousand miles seems pretty far, but | they've got planes and trains and cars. I'd | walk to you if I had no other |

| Bm | Bm/A | G | A |

way. Our | friends would all make fun of us and | we'll just laugh along because we |

| D5 | D5/C# | Bm | Bm/A | G |

know that none of them have felt this | way. De - | lilah, I can promise you that |

| A | Bm |

by the time that we get through, the | world will never ever be the | same, and you're to |

Verse

| A | A5 | D5 |

blame. | | 3. Hey there, Delilah, you be |

| F#m | D5 | F#m |

good and don't you miss me. Two more | years and you'll be done with school and | I'll be makin' hist'ry like I |

| Bm | Bm/A | G | A | Bm | Bm/A |

do. | You'll know it's all because of | you. |

| G | A | Bm | Bm/A | G | A |

We can do whatever we want | to. | Hey there, Delilah, here's to |

D.S. al Coda

| Bm | A | A5 |

you, this one's for | you. | |

⊕ Coda   **Outro** | 1. - 4. | 5. |

w/ Voc. ad lib.

| Bm | Bm/C# | D5 | D5/A | Bm | Bm/C# | D |

me, what you do to | me. | |

27

I Walk the Line

Words and Music by John R. Cash

To Coda 1 ⊕

%Verse

E   A

| ver - y,   ver - y | eas - y   to   be | true. | | I   find   my - |
| way   to | keep   me   on   your | side. | | You   give   me |

E   A

| self   a - | lone   when   each   day's | through. | | Yes,   I'll   ad - |
| cause   for | love   that   I   can't | hide. | | For   you,   I |

D   A

| mit   that   even | I'm   a   fool   for | you. | | Be - cause   you're |
| know   I'd   e - ven | try   to   turn   the | tide. | | Be - cause   you're |

E   A

| mine, | I   walk   the | line. | | ‖
| mine, | I   walk   the | line. | |

Interlude

D   1.   2.

‖: | | | :‖   3. As   sure   as   ‖

Verse

A   D

| night   is | dark   and   day   is | light, | | I   keep   you |

A   D

| on   my | mind   both   day   and | night. | | And   hap - pi - |

G   D

| ness   I've | known   proves   that   it's | right. | | Be - cause   you're |

A   D

| mine, | I   walk   the | line. | | ‖

Interlude

A   *D.S. al Coda 1*

‖: | | :‖   4. You've   got   a   ‖

⊕ **Coda 1**

Interlude

E   *D.S.S. al Coda 2*

‖: | :‖   5. I   keep   a   ‖

⊕ **Coda 2**

Outro   *Repeat and fade*

‖: E | | :‖

29

I Won't Back Down

Words and Music by Tom Petty and Jeff Lynne

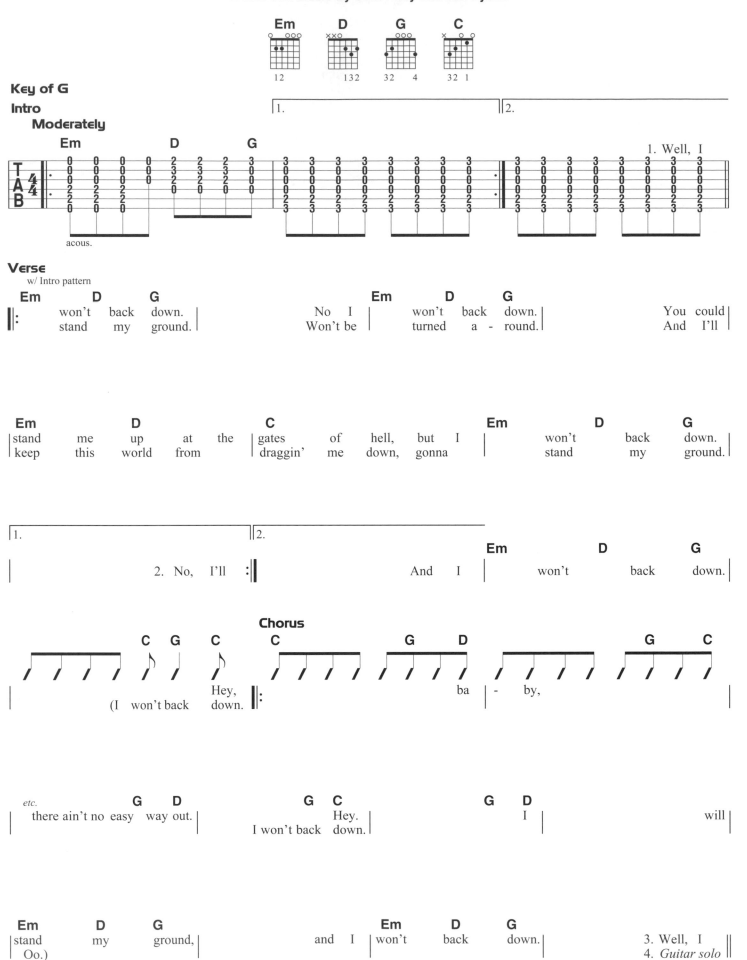

Verse

| Em | D | G | | | | Em | D | G | | |
know what's right. | I got | just one life | | | in a |

| Em | D | C | | Em | D | G |
world that keeps on | pushin' me around. But I'll | stand my ground, |

| | Em | D | G | | C G C | | C G C |
and I | won't back down. | Hey, | *Solo ends* | Hey, |
(I won't back down.) | (I won't back down.)

1. **2.**

Outro-Chorus

| C | G D | G C | G D | G C |
ba | - by, | there ain't no easy way out. | Hey. |
I won't back down.

| G D | Em D G | C G C |
I | won't back down. | Hey, |
Oo. | I won't back down.

| G D | G C | G D | G C |
ba | - by, | there ain't no easy way out. | Hey. |
I won't back down.

| G D | Em D G | and I |
I | will | stand my ground, |
Oo.

| Em D G | Em D *G |
won't back down. | No, I | won't back down. |
Oo.) |

*Let chord ring.

I Won't Give Up

Words and Music by Jason Mraz and Michael Natter

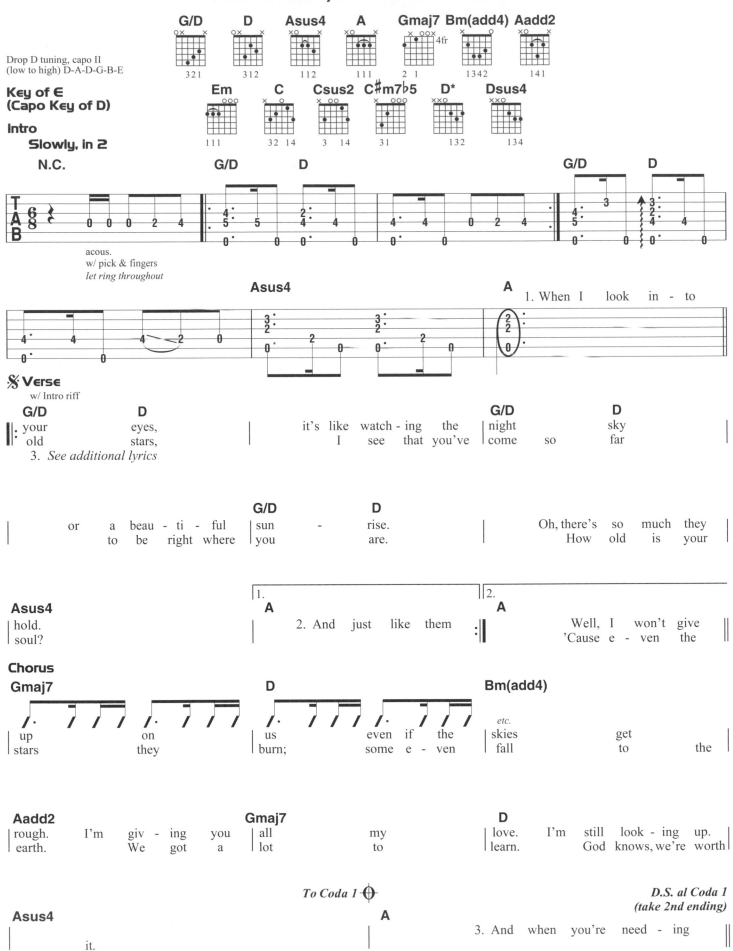

Drop D tuning, capo II
(low to high) D-A-D-G-B-E

Key of E
(Capo Key of D)

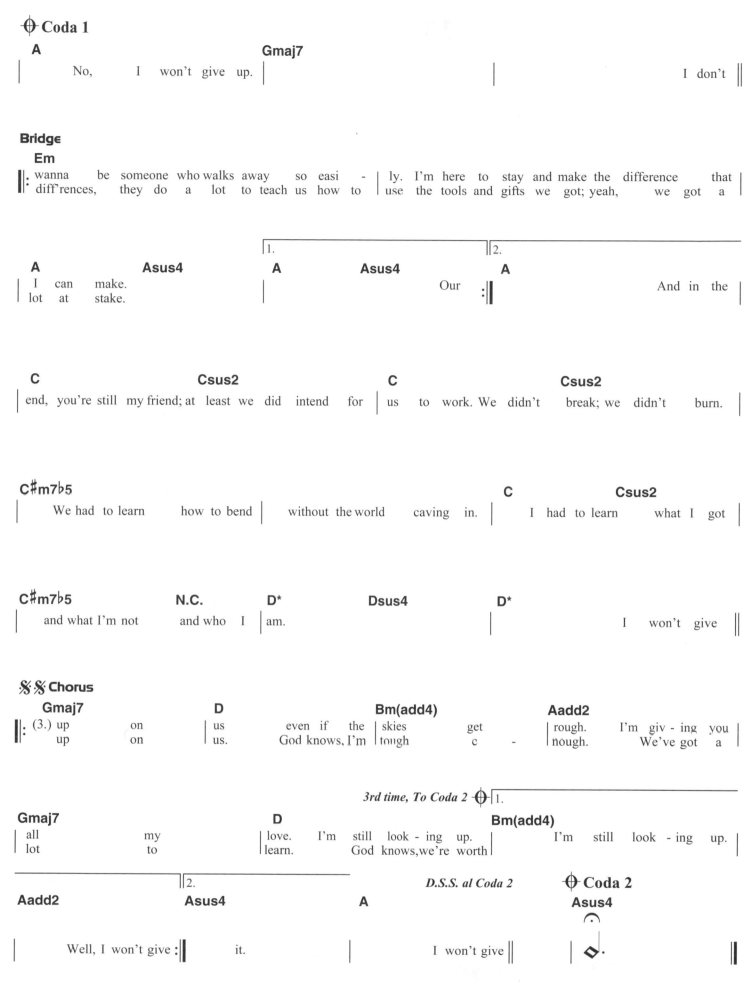

Additional Lyrics

3. And when you're needing your space to do some navigating
   I'll be here patiently waiting to see what you find.

Imagine

Words and Music by John Lennon

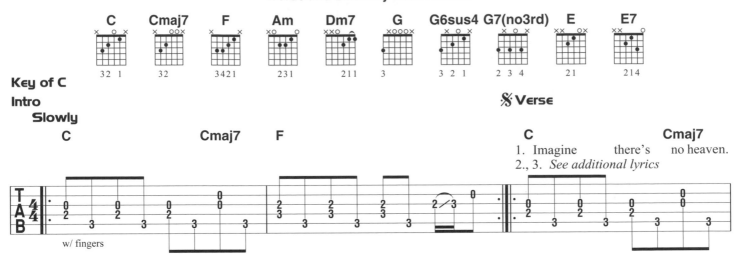

Key of C
Intro
Slowly

𝄋 **Verse**

1. Imagine   there's   no heaven.
2., 3. *See additional lyrics*

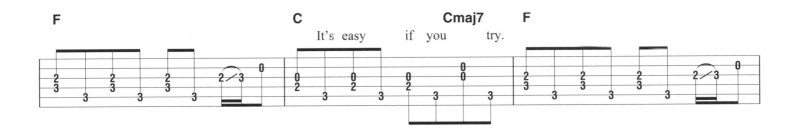

w/ fingers

It's easy   if you   try.

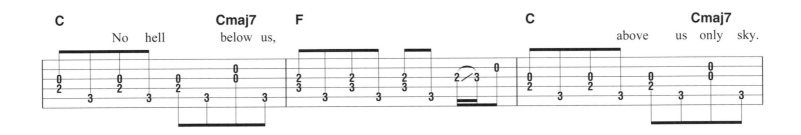

No   hell   below us,   above   us only sky.

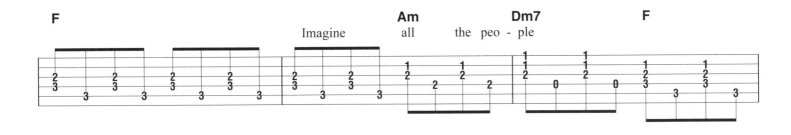

Imagine   all   the peo - ple

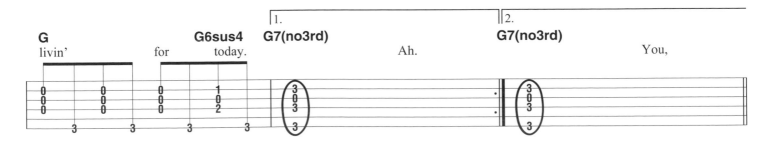

livin'   for   today.   Ah.   You,

Chorus

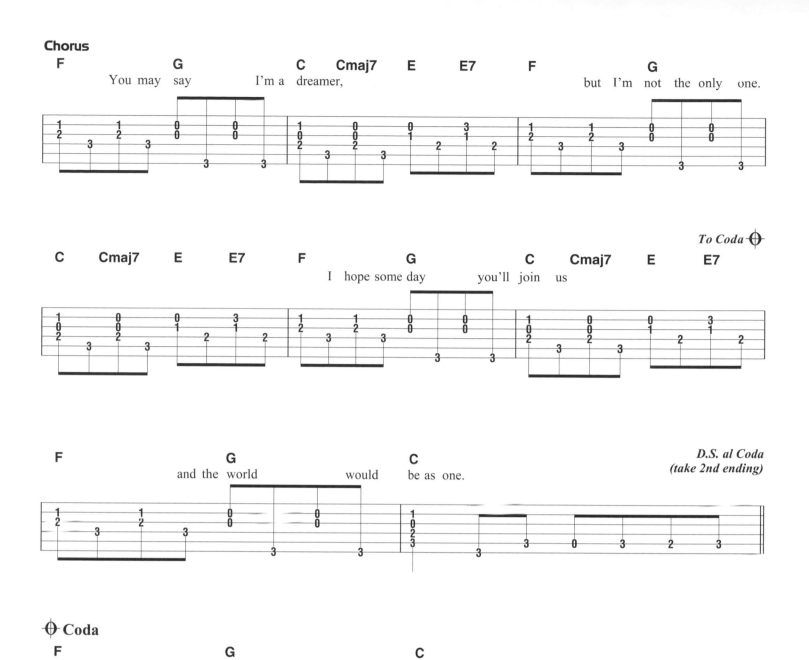

You may say I'm a dreamer, but I'm not the only one.

I hope some day you'll join us

To Coda ⊕

and the world would be as one.

D.S. al Coda
(take 2nd ending)

⊕ **Coda**

and the world will live as one.

rit.

Additional Lyrics

2. Imagine there's no countries.
It isn't hard to do.
Nothing to kill or die for,
And no religion too.
Imagine all the people livin' life in peace.

3. Imagine no possessions.
I wonder if you can.
No need for greed or hunger,
A brotherhood of man.
Imagine all the people sharing all the world.

Jamie's Cryin'

Words and Music by Edward Van Halen, Alex Van Halen, Michael Anthony and David Lee Roth

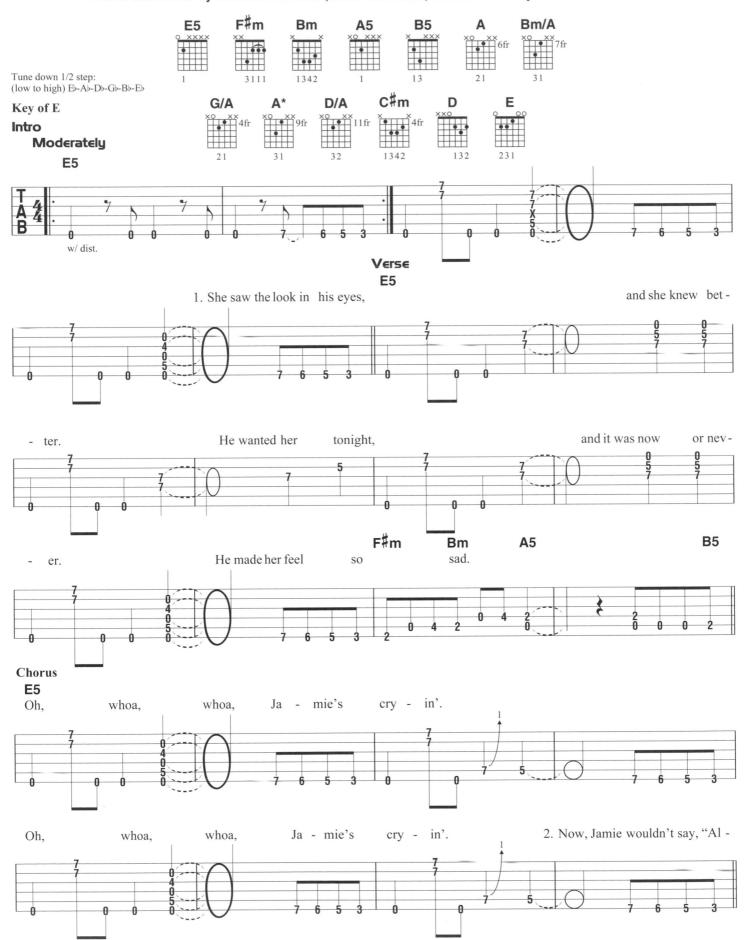

Tune down 1/2 step:
(low to high) E♭-A♭-D♭-G♭-B♭-E♭

Key of E

Intro

Moderately

w/ dist.

Verse

1. She saw the look in his eyes, and she knew bet-

-ter. He wanted her tonight, and it was now or nev-

-er. He made her feel so sad.

Chorus

Oh, whoa, whoa, Ja - mie's cry - in'.

Oh, whoa, whoa, Ja - mie's cry - in'. 2. Now, Jamie wouldn't say, "Al-

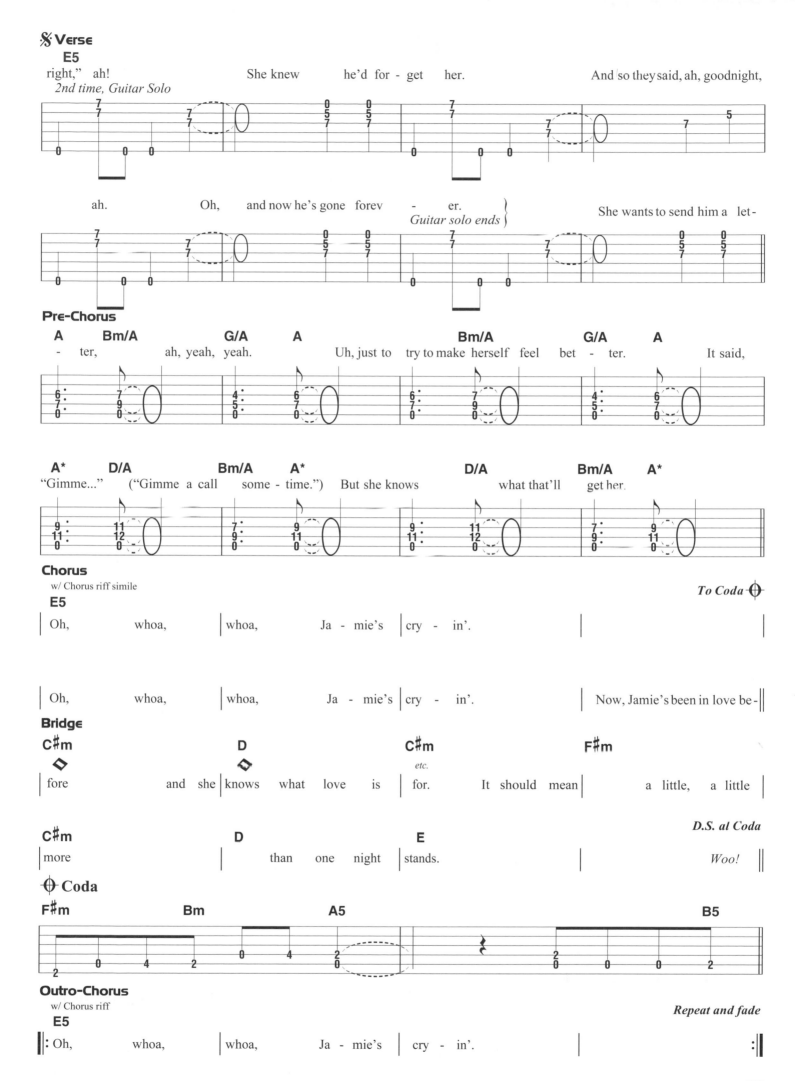

Jeremy

Music by Jeff Ament
Lyric by Eddie Vedder

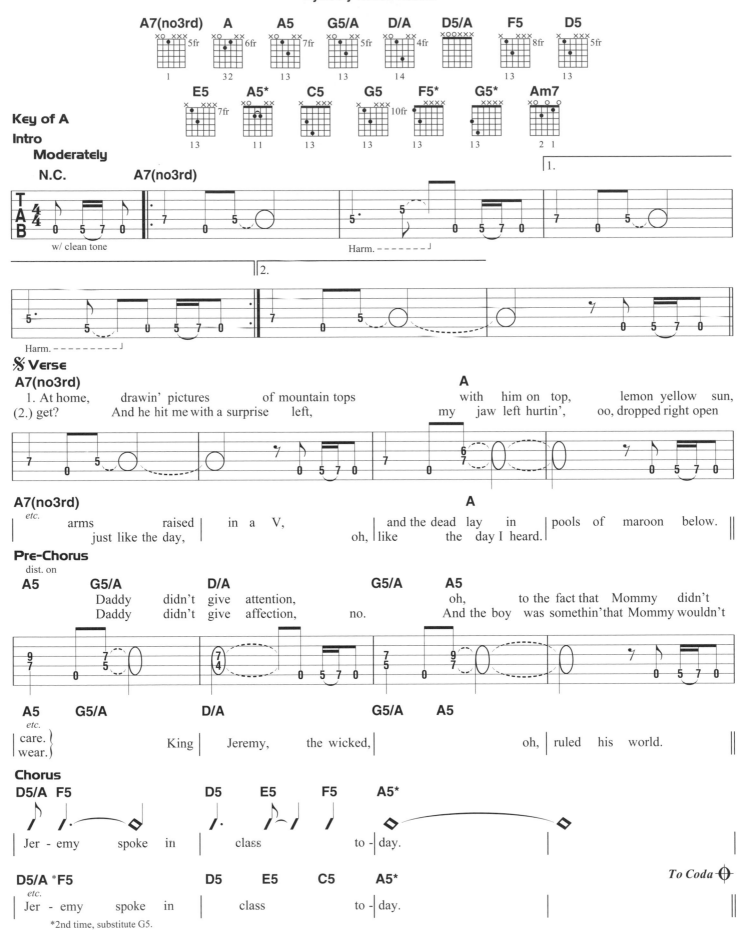

Verse
w/ Verse riff (dist. off)

A7(no3rd)   **A**

| 2. Clearly I remem - ber pickin' on the boy, | seemed a harmless | little fuck. |

A7(no3rd)   **A**   *D.S. al Coda*

| Mm, but we unleashed a | lion.   Gnashed his | teeth and bit the recess lady's | breast, how could I for- ‖

Coda
D5/A F5   **D5   E5   F5   A5***

| Jer - emy spoke in | class to - | day. | ‖

Bridge
A7(no3rd)

| Hoo, hoo, hoo, hoo, hoo, hoo, hoo, hoo. | hoo, hoo. Try to forget

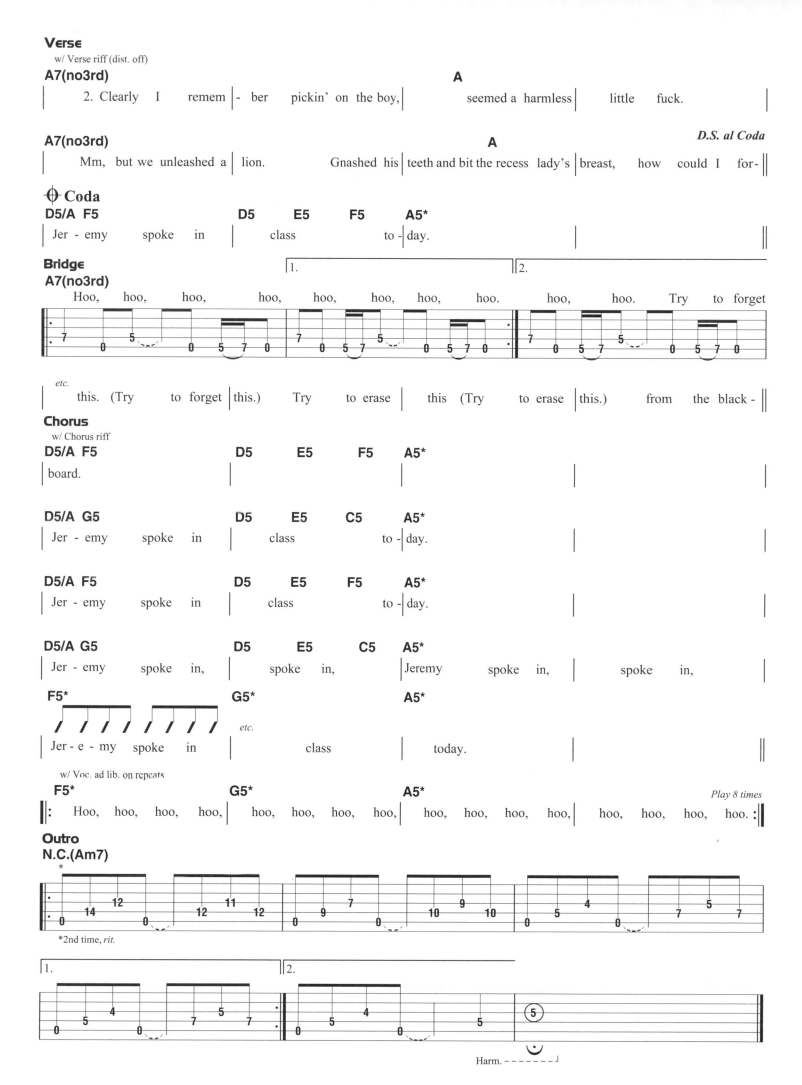

etc.

| this. (Try to forget | this.) Try to erase | this (Try to erase | this.) from the black- ‖

Chorus
w/ Chorus riff

D5/A F5   **D5   E5   F5   A5***

| board. | | | | |

D5/A G5   **D5   E5   C5   A5***

| Jer - emy spoke in | class to - | day. | | |

D5/A F5   **D5   E5   F5   A5***

| Jer - emy spoke in | class to - | day. | |

D5/A G5   **D5   E5   C5   A5***

| Jer - emy spoke in, | spoke in, | Jeremy spoke in, | spoke in, |

F5*   **G5***   **A5***

| Jer - e - my spoke in | class | today. | ‖

w/ Voc. ad lib. on repeats

F5*   **G5***   **A5***   *Play 8 times*

‖: Hoo, hoo, hoo, hoo, | hoo, hoo, hoo, hoo, | hoo, hoo, hoo, hoo, | hoo, hoo, hoo, hoo. :‖

Outro
N.C.(Am7)

2nd time, rit.

Harm. - - - - - - -

39

Jolene

Words and Music by Dolly Parton

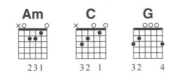

Capo IV

Key of C#m (Capo Key of Am)

Intro

Moderately

w/ pick & fingers

§ Chorus

lene,   Jo - lene,   Jo - lene, Jo - lene,   I'm

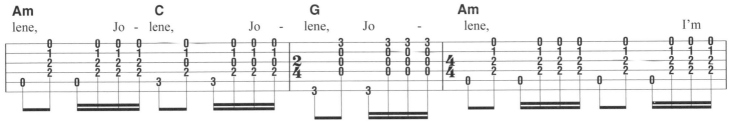

G   Am

begging of you, please don't take my | man.   Jo -

lene,   Jo - lene,   Jo - lene,   Jo - lene,

G   Am

please don't take him just because you | can.   1.Your

Verse

Am   C   G   Am   G

beauty is beyond compare, with | flaming locks of auburn hair, with | iv'ry skin and eyes of em'rald
2., 3. *See additional lyrics*

Am   C

green.   Your | smile is like a breath of spring, your

| **G** | **Am** | **G** | **Am** | *To Coda* ⊕ |

| voice is soft like summer rain, and | I cannot compete with you, | Jolene. | | |

| 1. | 2. | *D.S. al Coda* | ⊕ **Coda** |

| | 2. He :‖ | Jo - ‖ | | Jo - ‖ |

Chorus

| **Am** | **C** | **G** | **Am** | |

| lene, | Jo - lene, | Jo - $\frac{2}{4}$ lene, | Jo - $\frac{4}{4}$ lene, | I'm |

| **G** | **Am** | | |

| begging of you, please don't take my | man. | | Jo - |

| **C** | **G** | **Am** | |

| lene, Jo - lene, | Jo - $\frac{2}{4}$ lene, Jo - $\frac{4}{4}$ lene, | | |

| **G** | **Am** | | |

| please don't take him even though you | can. | | ‖ |

Outro

w/ Intro riff

Repeat and fade

‖: **Am** | :‖

Additional Lyrics

2. He talks about you in his sleep
And there's nothing I can do to keep
From cryin' when he calls your name, Jolene.
And I can eas'ly understand
How you could eas'ly take my man,
But you don't know what he means to me, Jolene.

3. You could have your choice of men,
But I could never love again.
He's the only one for me, Jolene.
I had to have this talk with you,
My happiness depends on you
And whatever you decide to do, Jolene.

Losing My Religion

Words and Music by William Berry, Peter Buck, Michael Mills and Michael Stipe

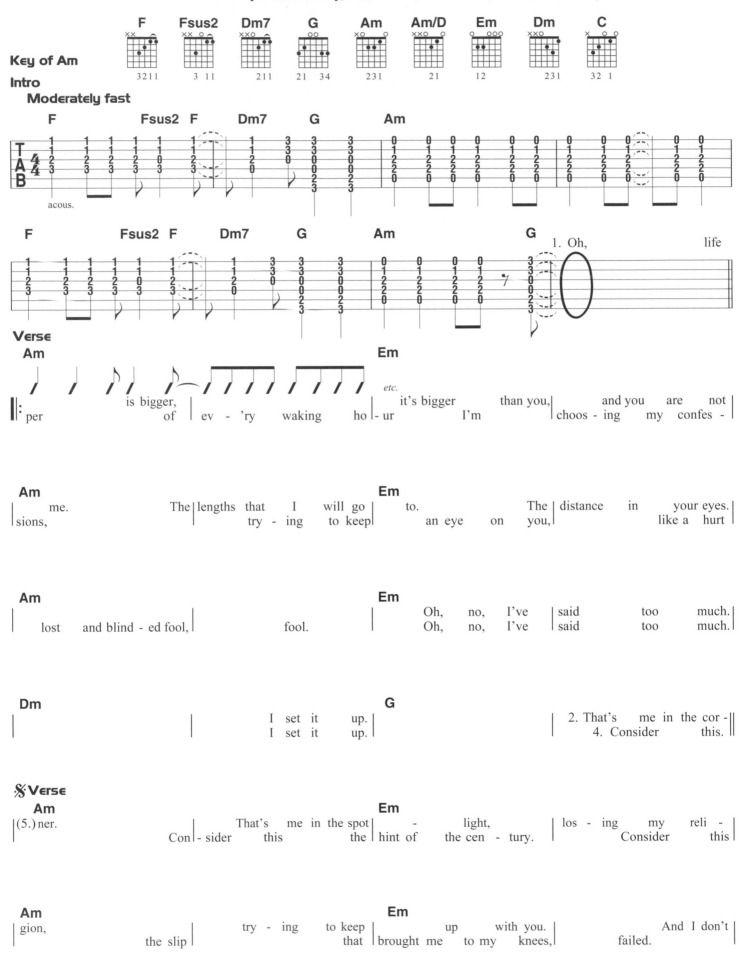

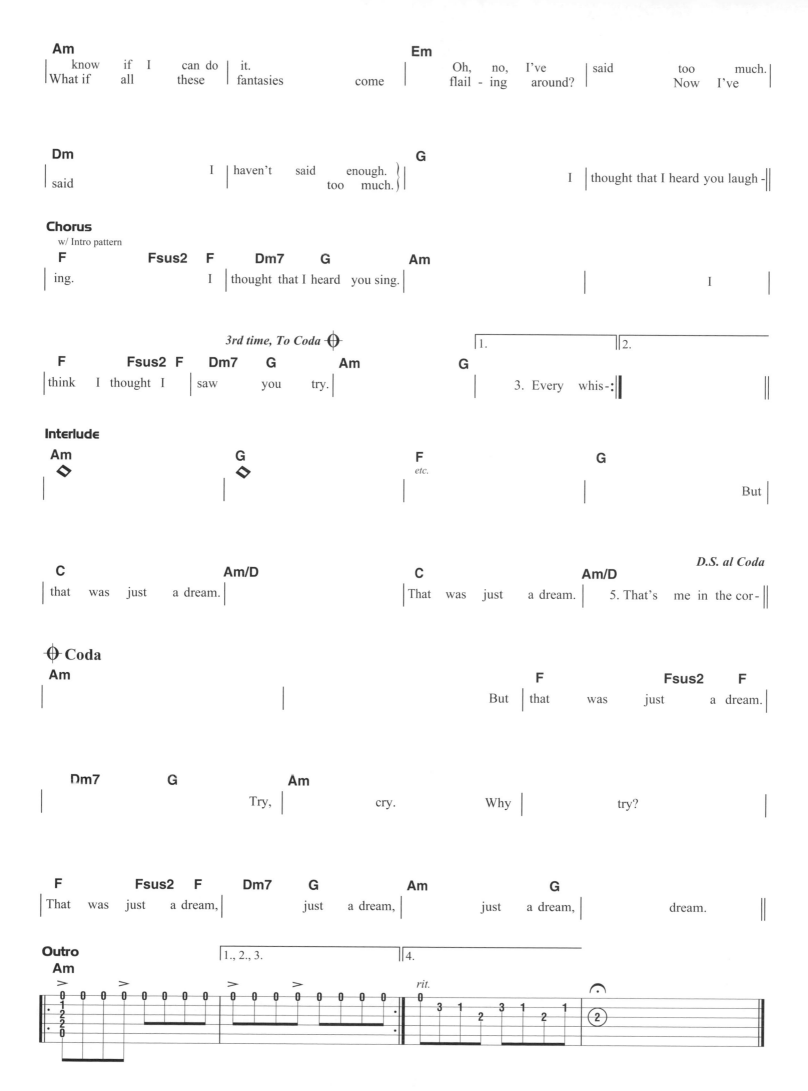

Am

know if I can do it.
What if all these fantasies come

Em

Oh, no, I've said too much.
flail - ing around? Now I've

Dm

said I haven't said enough.
too much.

G

I thought that I heard you laugh -

Chorus

w/ Intro pattern

F Fsus2 F Dm7 G Am

ing. I thought that I heard you sing. I

3rd time, To Coda ⊕

F Fsus2 F Dm7 G Am

think I thought I saw you try.

G

1.

2.

G

3. Every whis -:

Interlude

Am G F G

etc.

But

C Am/D C Am/D

D.S. al Coda

that was just a dream.
That was just a dream. 5. That's me in the cor -

⊕ **Coda**

Am

F Fsus2 F

But that was just a dream.

Dm7 G Am

Try, cry. Why try?

F Fsus2 F Dm7 G Am G

That was just a dream, just a dream, just a dream, dream.

Outro

1., 2., 3.

4.

Am

rit.

43

Louie, Louie

Words and Music by Richard Berry

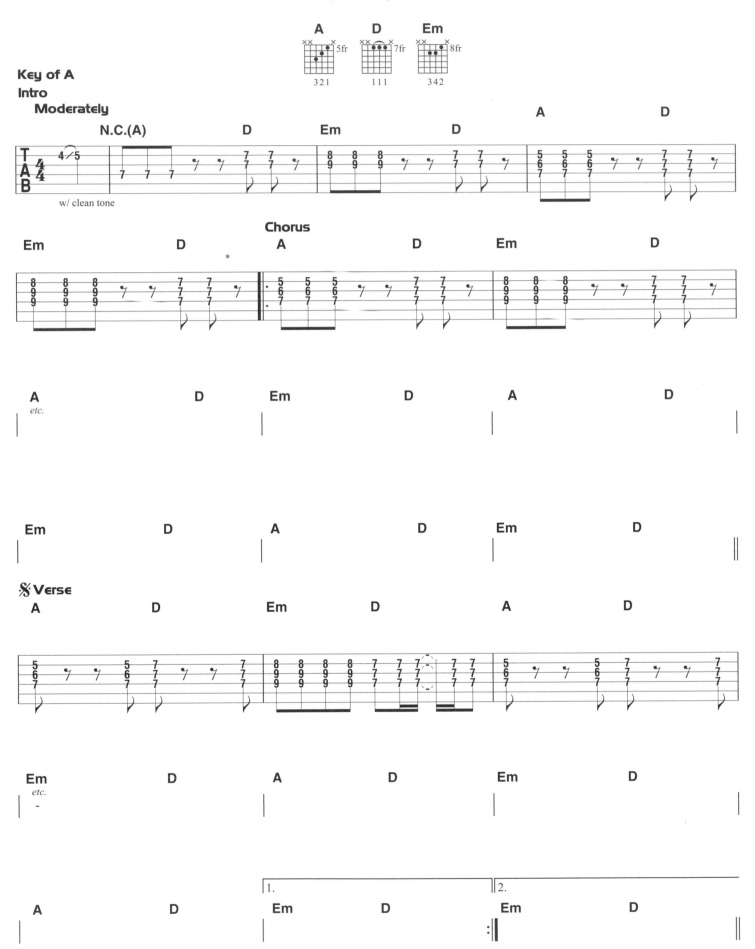

Chorus
w/ Chorus pattern

A	D	Em	D	A	D

Em	D	A	D	Em	D

To Coda ⊕   **Guitar Solo**

A	D	Em	D	‖: A	D

4th time, D.S. al Coda
(take 2nd ending)

Em	D	A	D	Em	D	:‖

⊕ **Coda**

Em	D	A	D	Em	D

A	D	Em	D	A N.C.	‖

More Than a Feeling

Words and Music by Tom Scholz

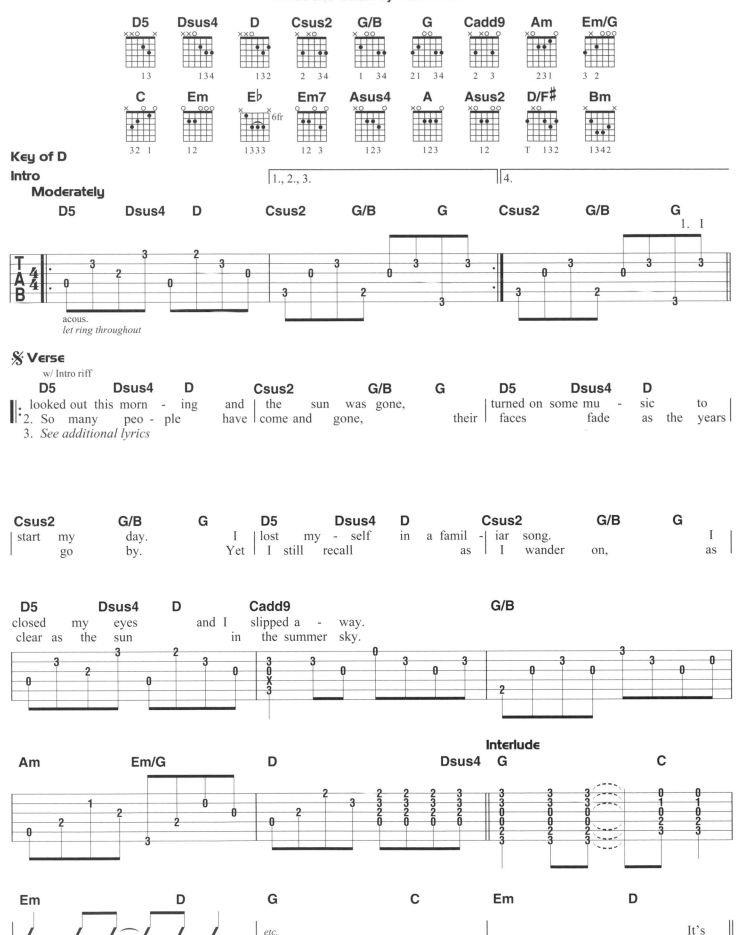

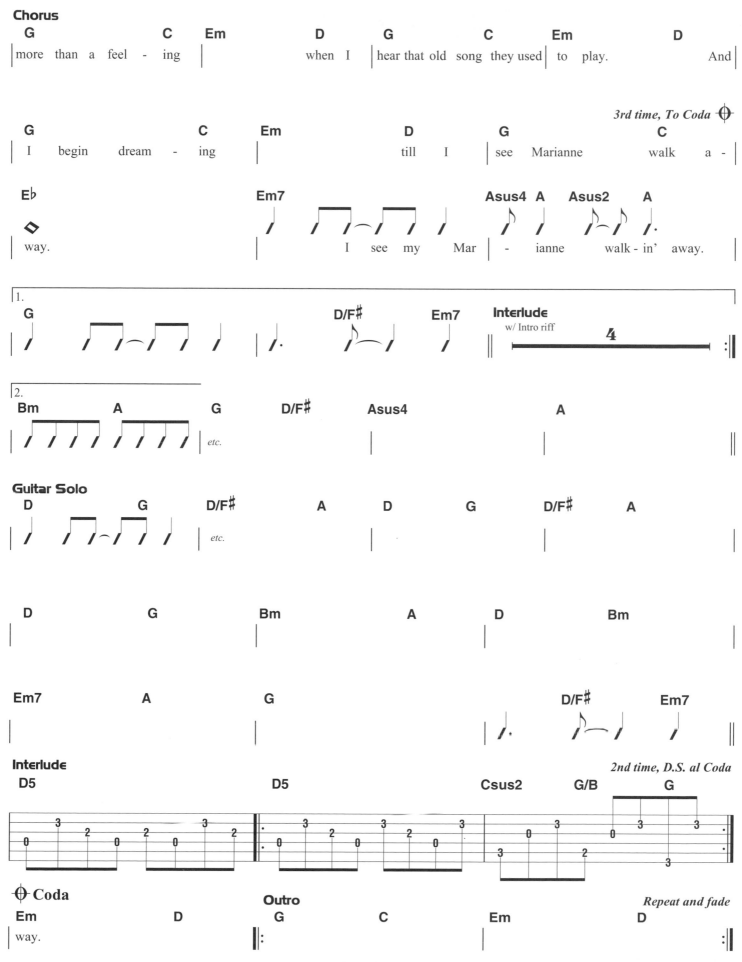

Additional Lyrics

3. When I'm tired and thinking cold,
   I hide in my music, forget the day
   And dream of a girl I used to know.
   I closed my eyes and she slipped away.

My Generation

Words and Music by Peter Townshend

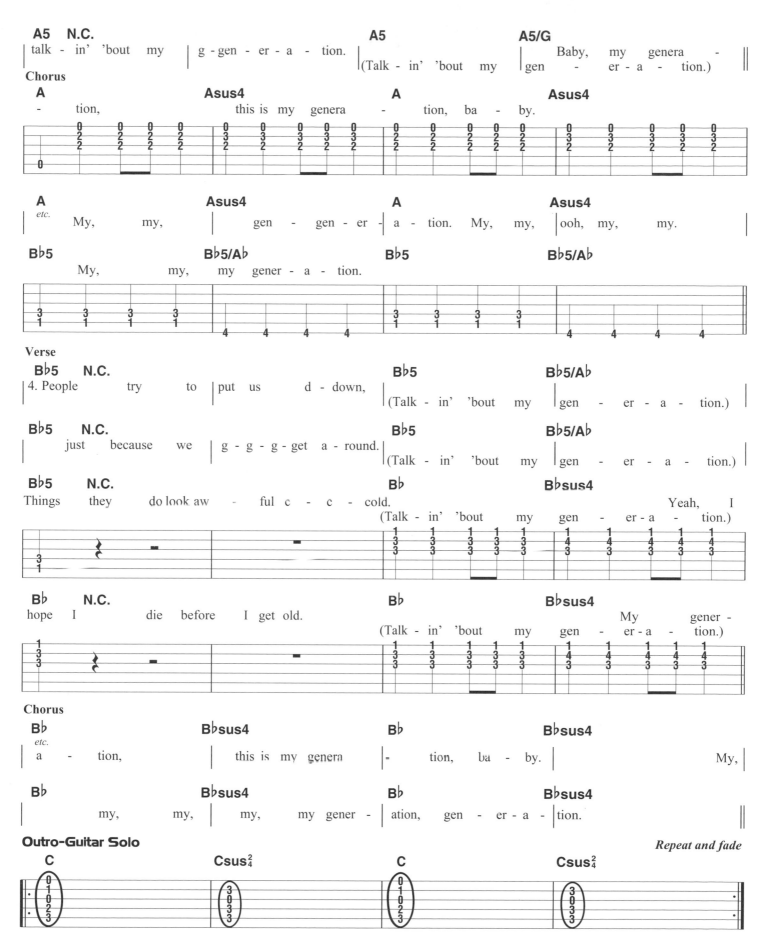

No One Knows

Words and Music by Mark Lanegan, Josh Homme and Nick Oliveri

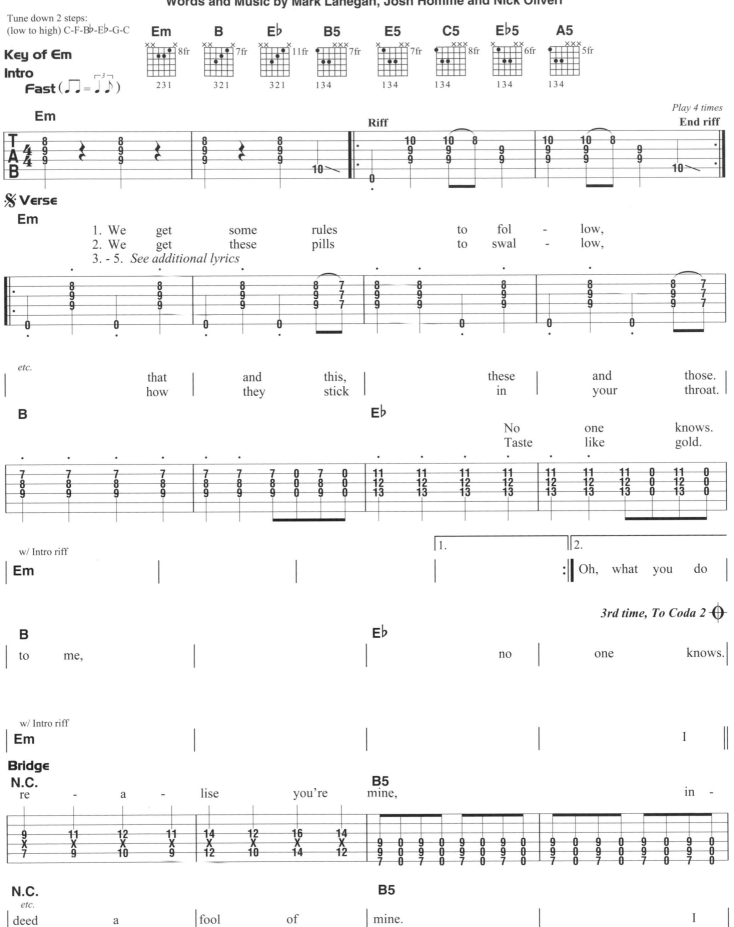

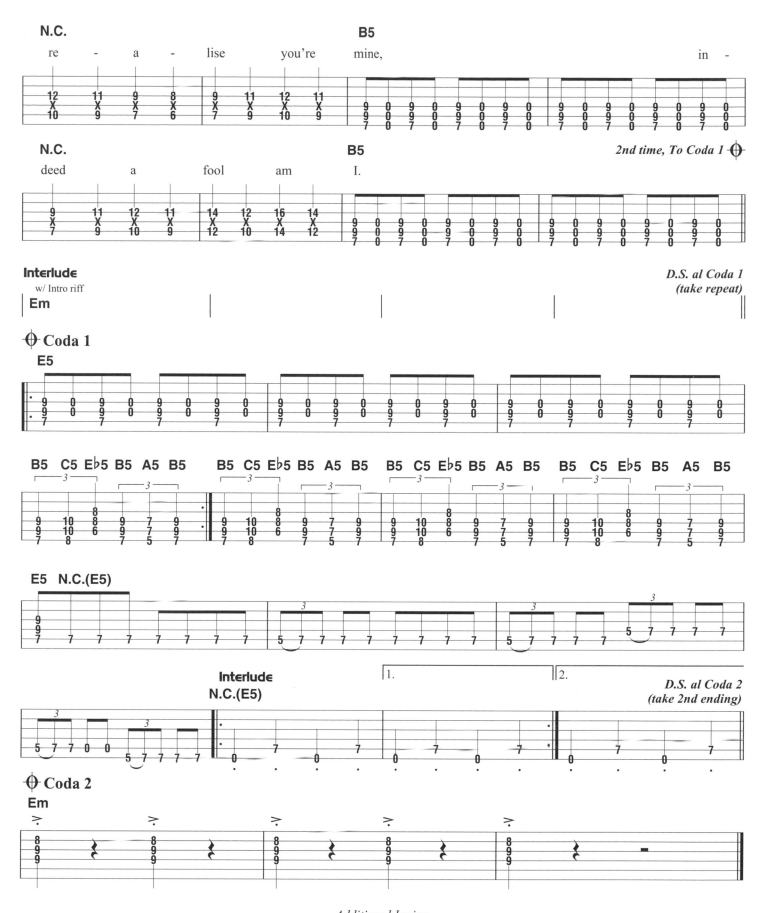

Additional Lyrics

3. I journey through the desert
   Of the mind with no hope.
   I follow.

4. I drift along the ocean,
   Dead lifeboats in the sun.
   And come undone.
   Pleasantly caving in,
   I come undone.

5. Heaven smiles above me,
   What a gift here below.
   But no one knows.
   The gift that you give to me,
   No one knows.

Paranoid

Words and Music by Anthony Iommi, John Osbourne, William Ward and Terence Butler

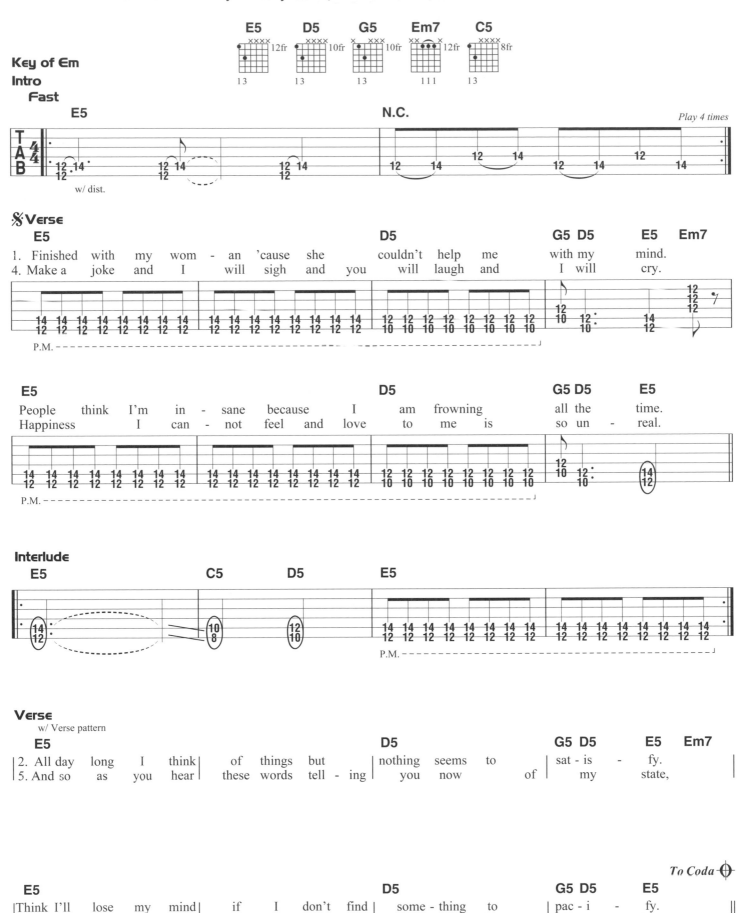

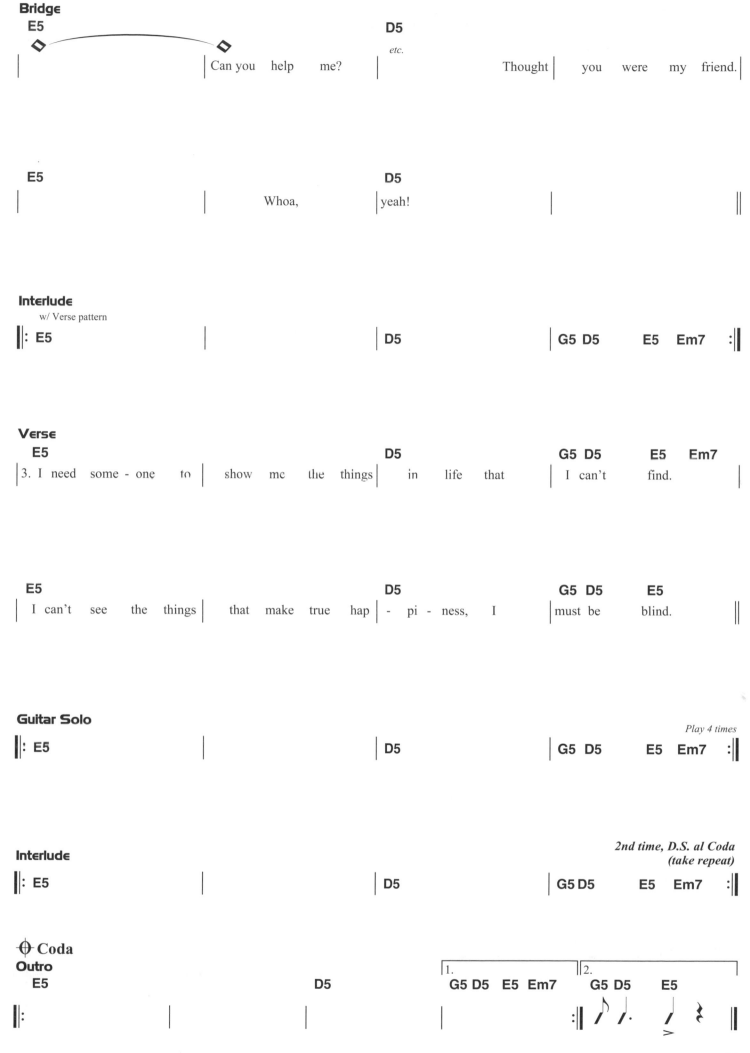

Bridge

E5   D5

                                         etc.

Can you help me?   Thought you were my friend.

E5   D5

Whoa,   yeah!

Interlude
w/ Verse pattern

‖: E5   D5   G5 D5   E5   Em7 :‖

Verse

E5   D5   G5 D5   E5   Em7

3. I need some - one to | show me the things | in life that | I can't find. |

E5   D5   G5 D5   E5

I can't see the things | that make true hap | - pi - ness, I | must be blind. ‖

Guitar Solo

                                                   Play 4 times

‖: E5   D5   G5 D5   E5   Em7 :‖

                                         2nd time, D.S. al Coda
                                         (take repeat)

Interlude

‖: E5   D5   G5 D5   E5   Em7 :‖

Ⓒ **Coda**
Outro

E5   D5   1. G5 D5 E5 Em7   2. G5 D5   E5

‖:   :‖ ‖

Patience

Words and Music by W. Axl Rose, Slash, Izzy Stradlin', Duff McKagan and Steven Adler

Tune down 1/2 step:
(low to high) Eb-Ab-Db-Gb-Bb-Eb

Key of G

Intro

Moderately

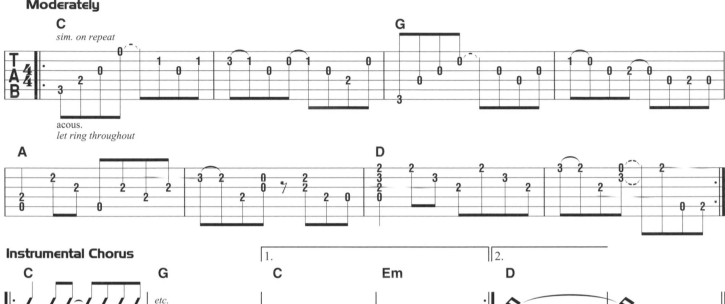

Instrumental Chorus

Verse

w/ Intro riff

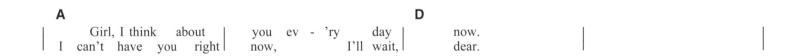

C
1. Shed a tear 'cause I'm | missin' you. | I'm still alright to smile. |
2. I sit here | on the stairs 'cause I'd | rather be alone. | If |

A   D
Girl, I think about | you ev - 'ry day | now. |
I can't have you right | now, I'll wait, | dear. |

C   G
Was a time when I | wasn't sure, but you | set my mind at ease. |
Some - times I | get so tense, but I | can't speed up the time. | But |

A   D
There is no doubt | you're in my heart | now. |
you know, love, there's one | more thing to consid | - er. |

§ Chorus

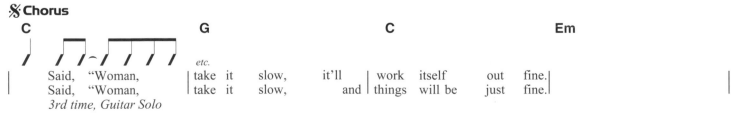

C   G   C   Em
Said, "Woman, | take it slow, it'll | work itself out fine. |
Said, "Woman, | take it slow, and | things will be just fine. |
3rd time, Guitar Solo

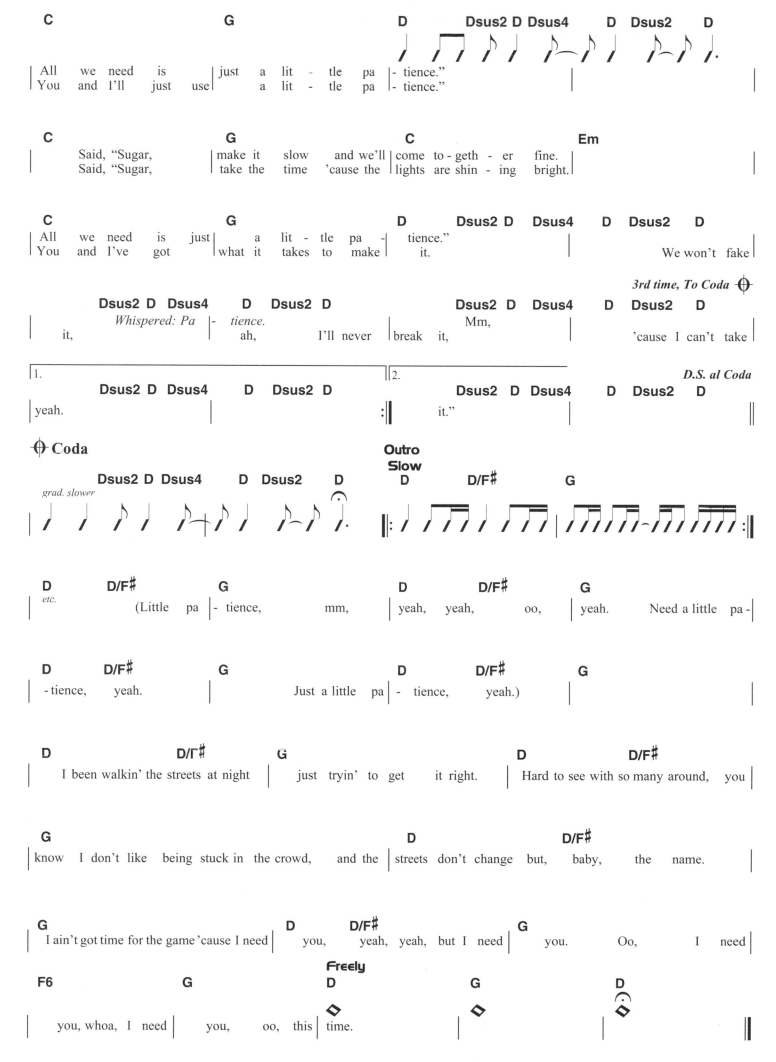

Photograph

Words and Music by Ed Sheeran and John McDaid

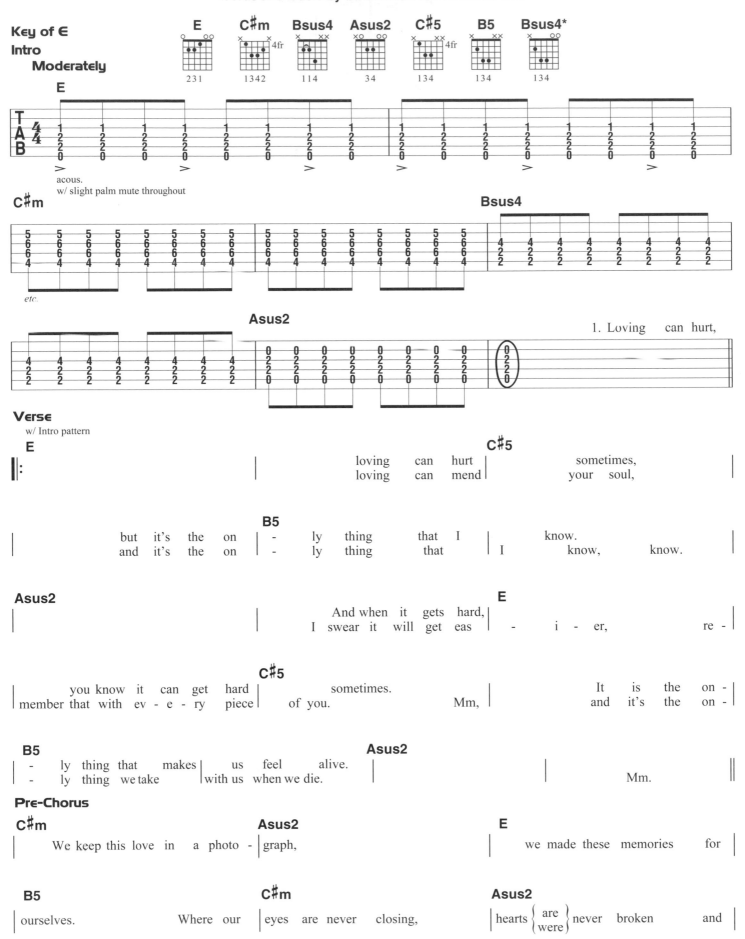

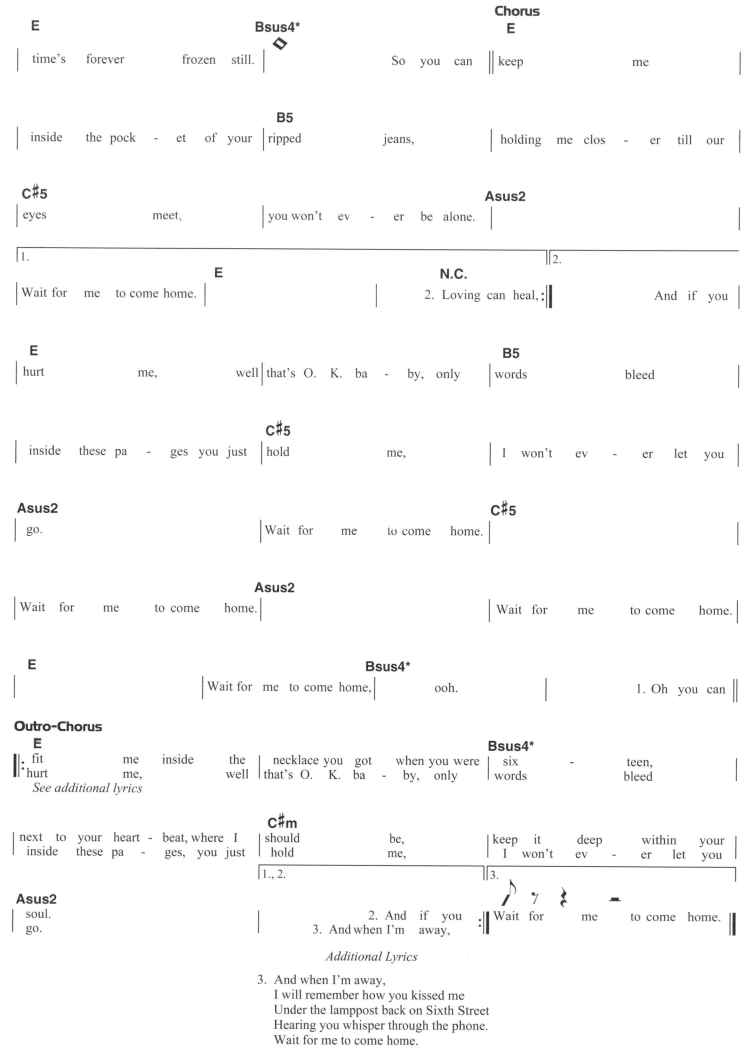

Plush

Words and Music by Scott Weiland, Dean DeLeo, Robert DeLeo and Eric Kretz

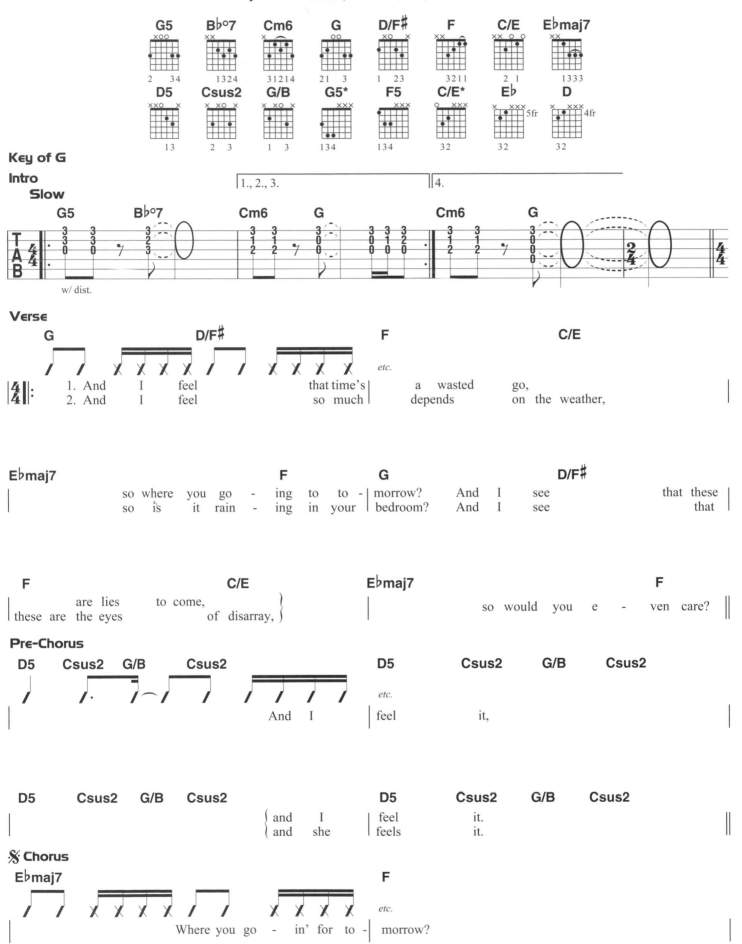

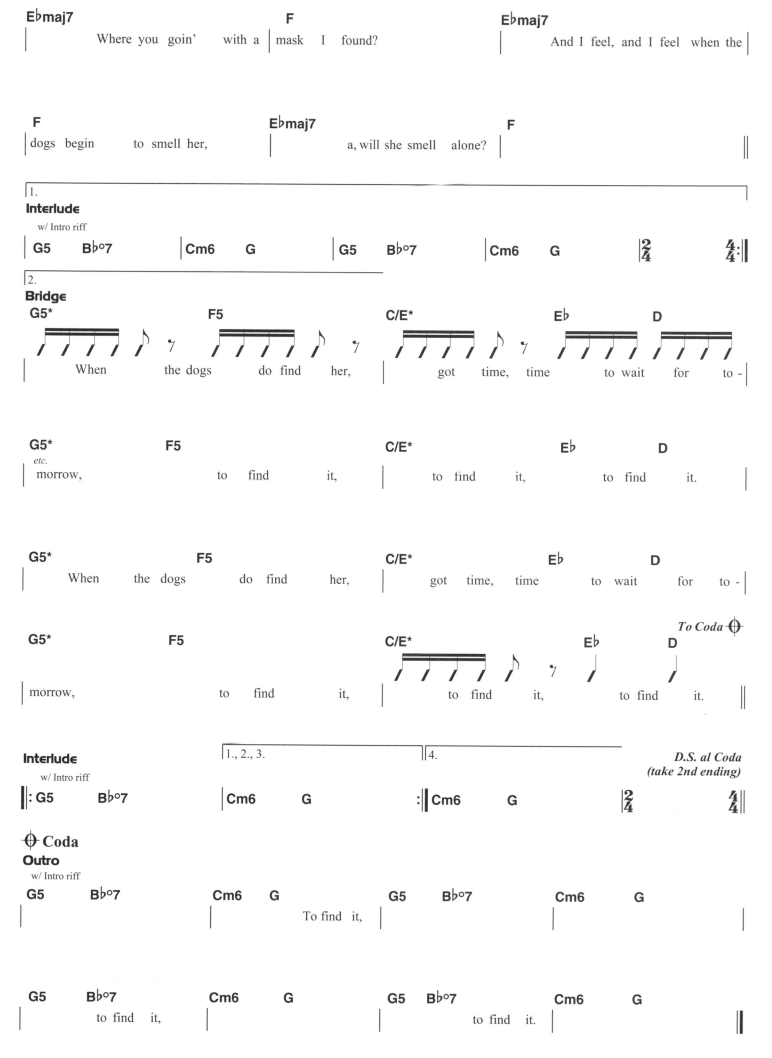

E♭maj7   **F**   **E♭maj7**

Where you goin' with a | mask I found? | And I feel, and I feel when the

F   **E♭maj7**   **F**

dogs begin to smell her, | a, will she smell alone? |

1.

Interlude
w/ Intro riff

| G5   B♭°7 | Cm6   G | G5   B♭°7 | Cm6   G   **2/4**   **4/4** :|

2.

Bridge

G5*   **F5**   **C/E***   **E♭**   **D**

When the dogs do find her,   got time, time to wait for to -

G5*   **F5**   **C/E***   **E♭**   **D**
etc.

morrow,   to find it,   to find it,   to find it.

G5*   **F5**   **C/E***   **E♭**   **D**

When the dogs do find her,   got time, time to wait for to -

To Coda ⊕

G5*   **F5**   **C/E***   **E♭**   **D**

morrow,   to find it,   to find it,   to find it.

Interlude   **1., 2., 3.**   **4.**   *D.S. al Coda*
   w/ Intro riff   *(take 2nd ending)*

‖: G5   B♭°7 | Cm6   G   :‖ Cm6   G   **2/4**   **4/4**‖

⊕ **Coda**

Outro
   w/ Intro riff

G5   B♭°7   Cm6   G   G5   B♭°7   Cm6   G

                            To find it, |

G5   B♭°7   Cm6   G   G5   B♭°7   Cm6   G

      to find it,   to find it.   ‖

Proud Mary

Words and Music by John Fogerty

C   A   G   F   D   Bm

Key of D

Intro

Moderately

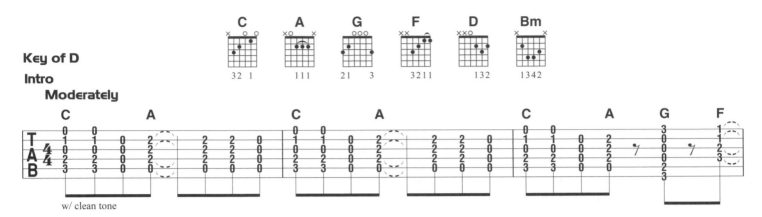

w/ clean tone

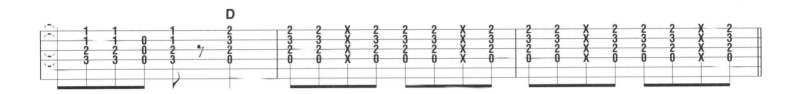

Verse

D

etc.

1. Left a good job in the cit - y,		workin' for the man ev'ry
2. Cleaned a lot of plates in Mem - phis,		pumped a lot of pain down in
3. If you come down to the riv - er,		bet you're gonna find some peo-

night and day	and I never lost one min - ute of sleep - in',	
New Or - leans	but I never saw the good side of the city	
- ple who live.	You don't have to worry 'cause you have no money,	

Pre-Chorus

A

worryin' 'bout the way things	might have been.	Big wheel keep on turn -
till I hitched a ride on a	river boat queen.	
people on a river are hap - py to give.		

3rd time, To Coda ⊕

Bm

- in',	Proud	Mary keep on burn	- in'.	Roll -

Chorus

D

- in',	roll	- in',	roll	- in' on a riv - er.	

Interlude
w/ Intro pattern

| C | A | | C | A | | C | A | G | F |

| | | D | | | | | | |

Guitar Solo

‖: D | | | | :‖

| A | | | Bm | | | Roll - ‖

Chorus
D

D.C. al Coda

| - in', roll | - in', roll | - in' on a riv - er. | | ‖

✦ **Coda**
Outro-Chorus
D

Repeat and fade

‖: - in', roll | - in', roll | - in' on a riv - er. | Roll - :‖

Rebel, Rebel

Words and Music by David Bowie

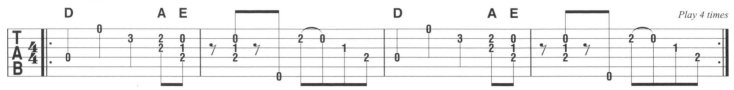

Key of A

Intro

Moderately

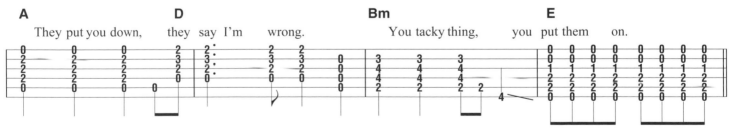

Play 4 times

Verse

w/ Intro riff

D	A E	D	A E
1., 2. You got your mother	in a whirl,	she's not sure if you're a	boy or a girl.

D	A E	D	A E
Hey, babe, your	hair's alright.	Hey, babe, let's	go { out / stay } tonight.

D	A E	D	A E
You like me and I	like it all.	We like dancing and we	look divine.

D	A E	D	A E
You love bands when they	play it hard.	You want more and you	want it fast.

Pre-Chorus

A	D	Bm	E
They put you down, they say I'm wrong.		You tacky thing, you put them on.	

Chorus

w/ Intro riff

D	A E	D	A E
Rebel, rebel, you've	torn your dress.	Rebel, rebel, your	face is a mess.

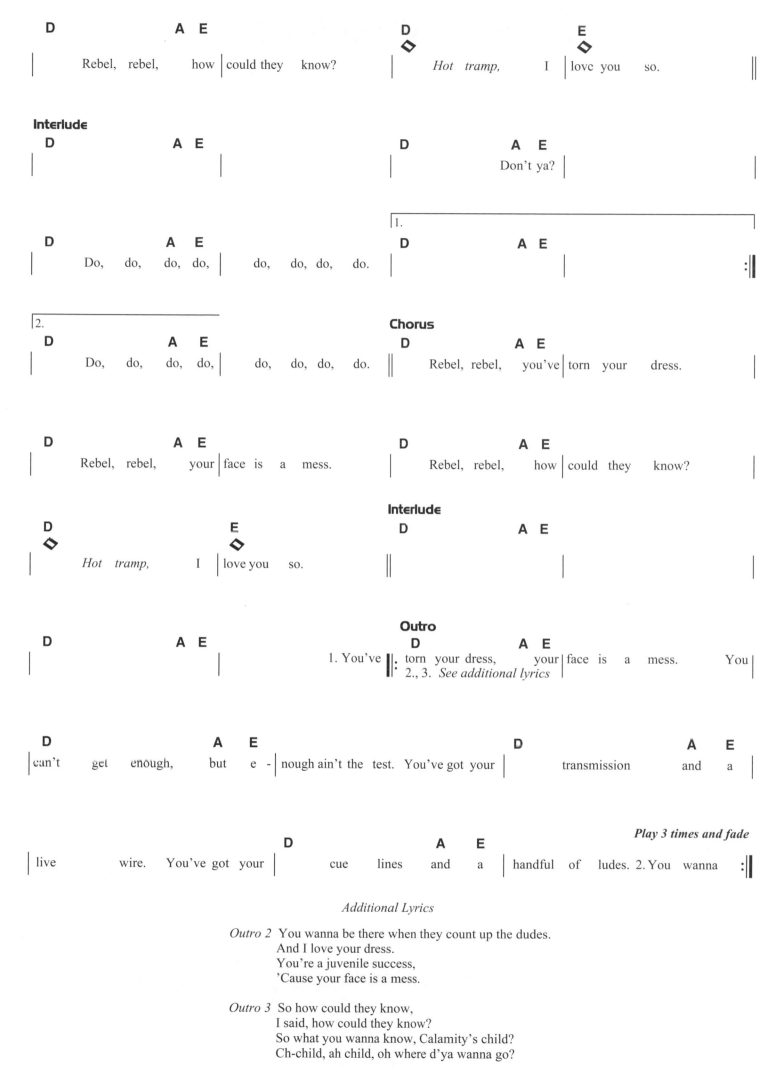

Additional Lyrics

Outro 2 You wanna be there when they count up the dudes.
And I love your dress.
You're a juvenile success,
'Cause your face is a mess.

Outro 3 So how could they know,
I said, how could they know?
So what you wanna know, Calamity's child?
Ch-child, ah child, oh where d'ya wanna go?

Redemption Song

Words and Music by Bob Marley

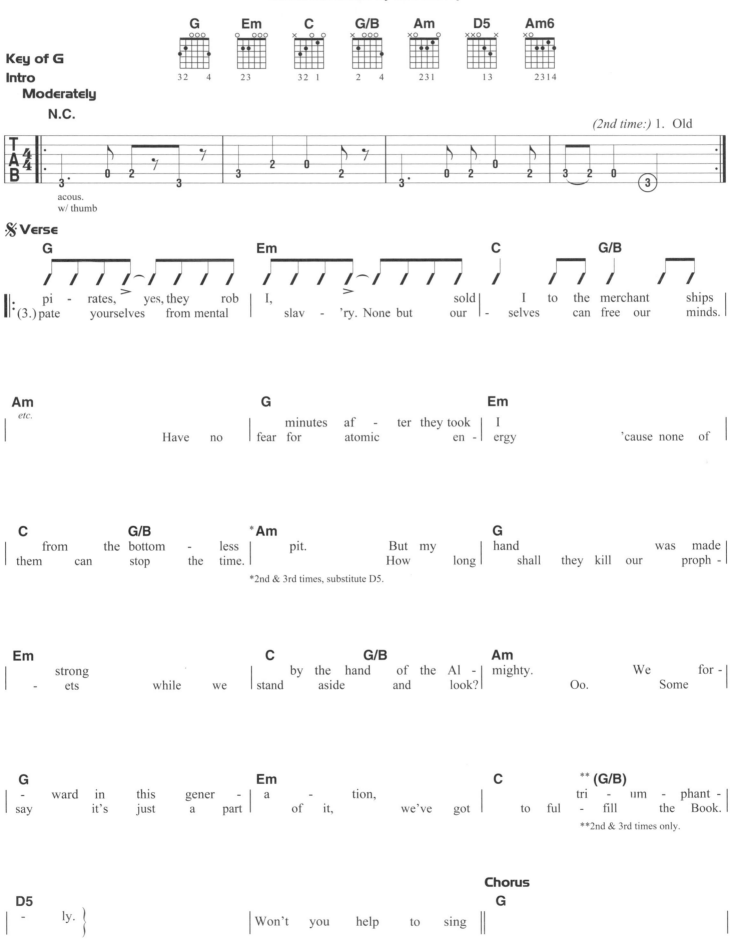

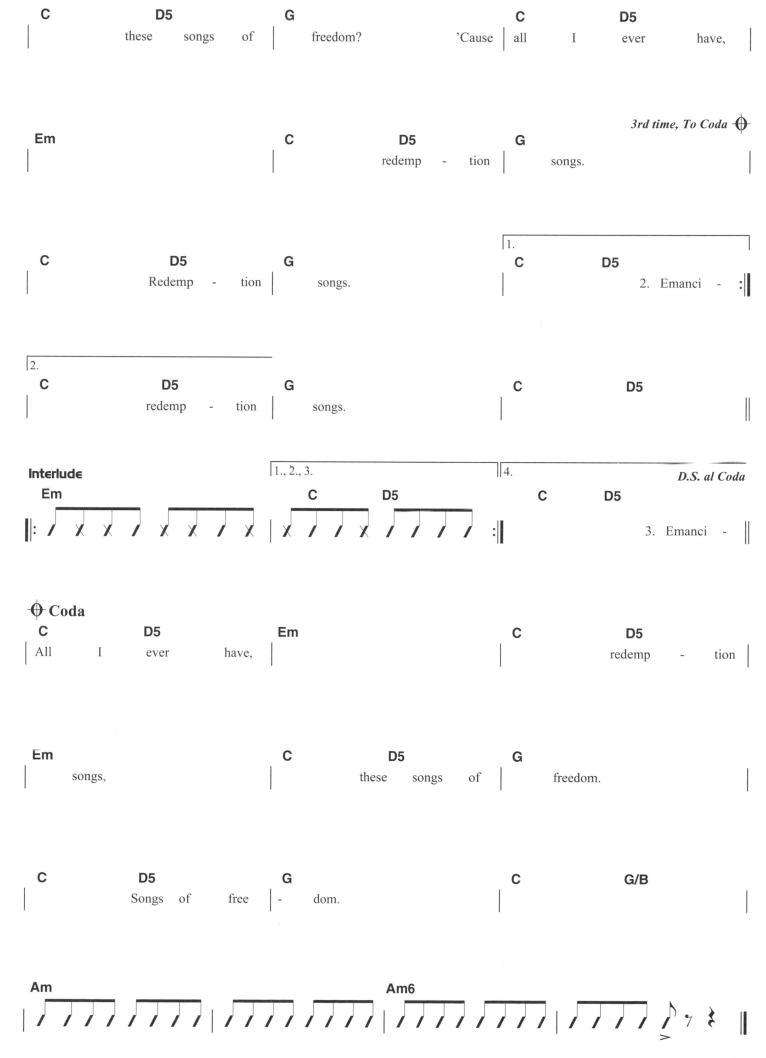

Riptide

Words and Music by Vance Joy

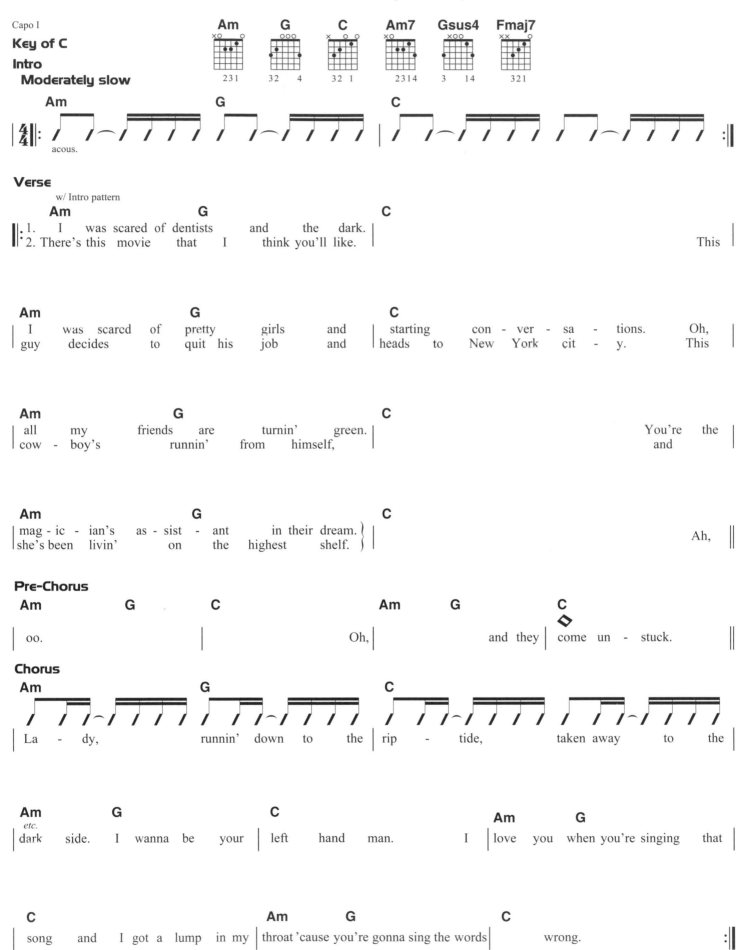

Interlude

N.C.(C)

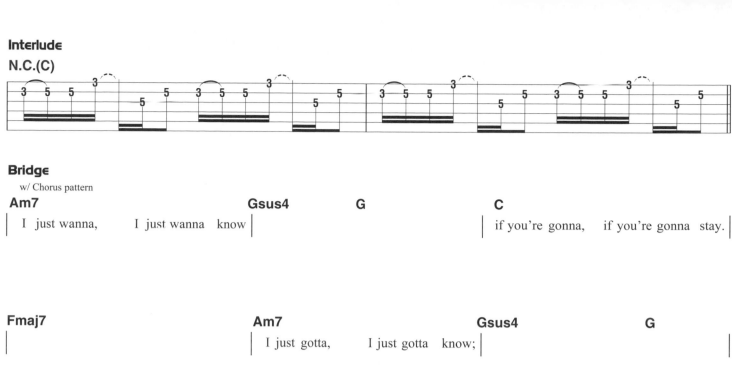

Bridge

w/ Chorus pattern

Am7		Gsus4	G		C
I just wanna,	I just wanna know			if you're gonna,	if you're gonna stay.

Fmaj7		Am7		Gsus4	G
		I just gotta,	I just gotta know;		

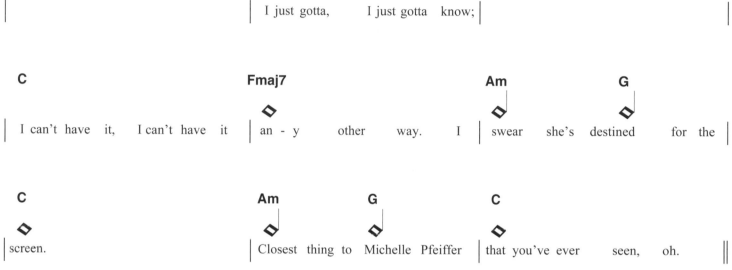

C		Fmaj7		Am	G
I can't have it,	I can't have it	an - y	other way. I	swear she's destined	for the

C		Am	G	C
screen.		Closest thing to Michelle Pfeiffer	that you've ever	seen, oh.

Chorus

w/ Chorus pattern

Am	G		C		Am	G
La - dy,	runnin' down to the	rip - tide, taken away	to the	dark side. I wanna	be your

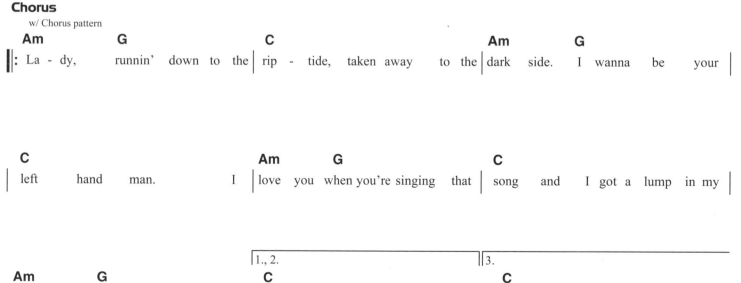

C		Am	G	C
left hand man. I	love you when you're singing that	song and I got a lump in my

1., 2.

3.

Am	G		C		C
throat 'cause you're gonna sing the words		wrong.		wrong, yeah. I got a lump in my

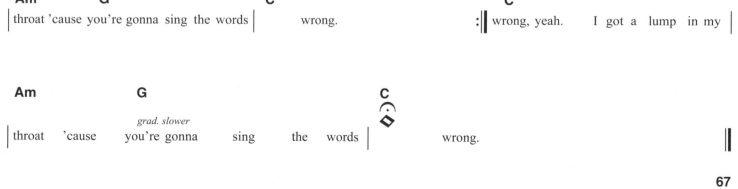

Am	G		C
throat	'cause you're gonna	sing the words	wrong.

grad. slower

Rock and Roll Never Forgets

Words and Music by Bob Seger

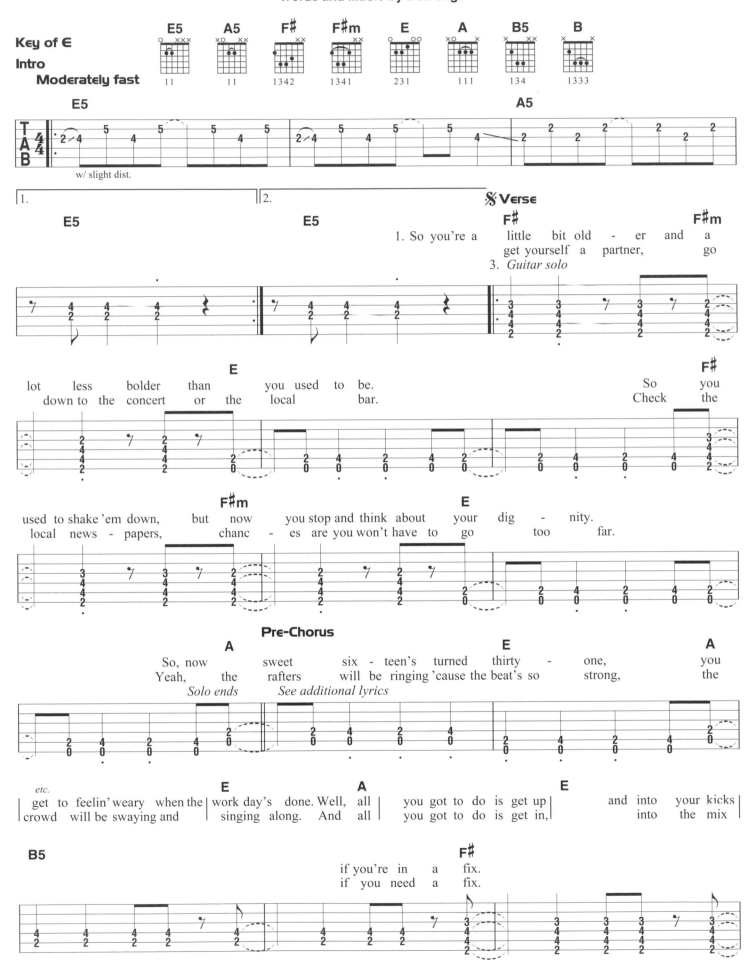

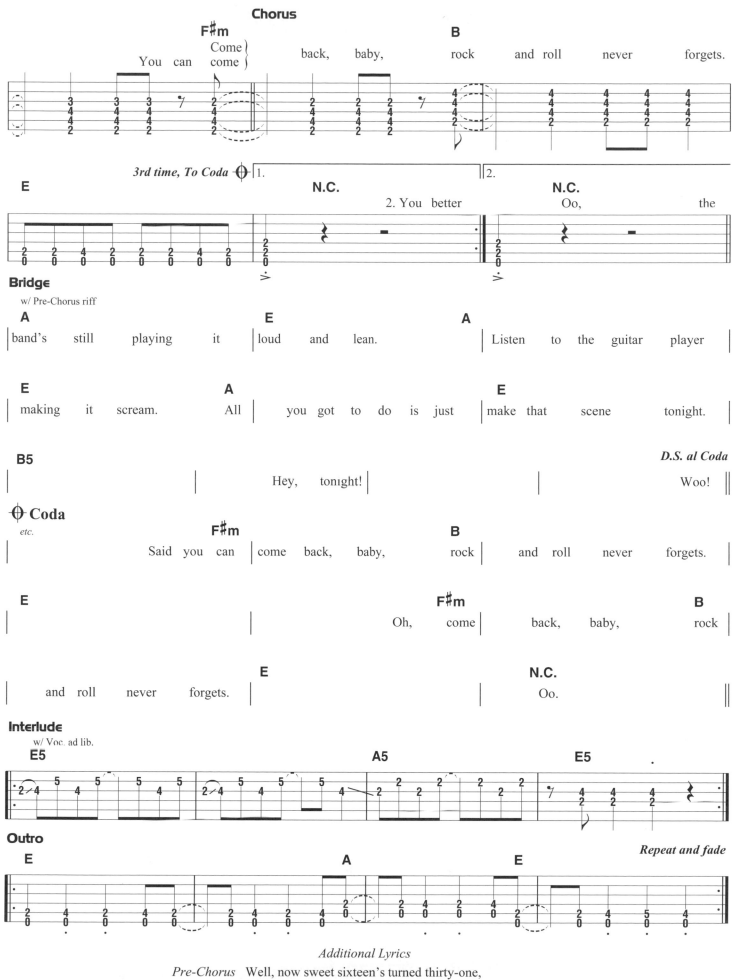

Additional Lyrics

Pre-Chorus Well, now sweet sixteen's turned thirty-one,
Feel a little tired, feeling under the gun.
Well, all of Chuck's children are out there playing his licks.
Get into your kicks,
Then come...

Safe & Sound

from THE HUNGER GAMES

Words and Music by Taylor Swift, T-Bone Burnett, John Paul White and Joy Williams

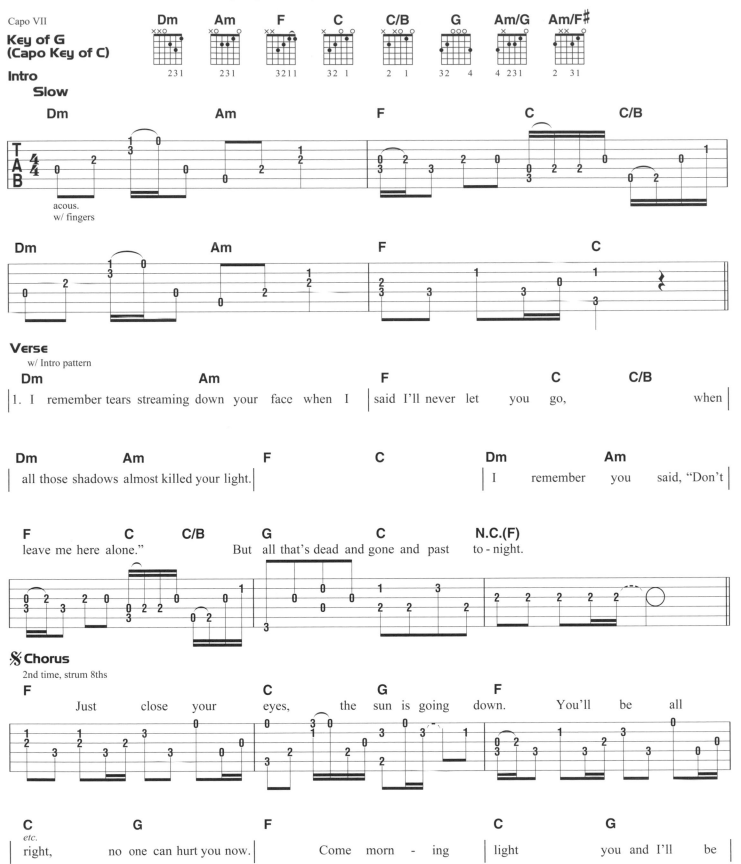

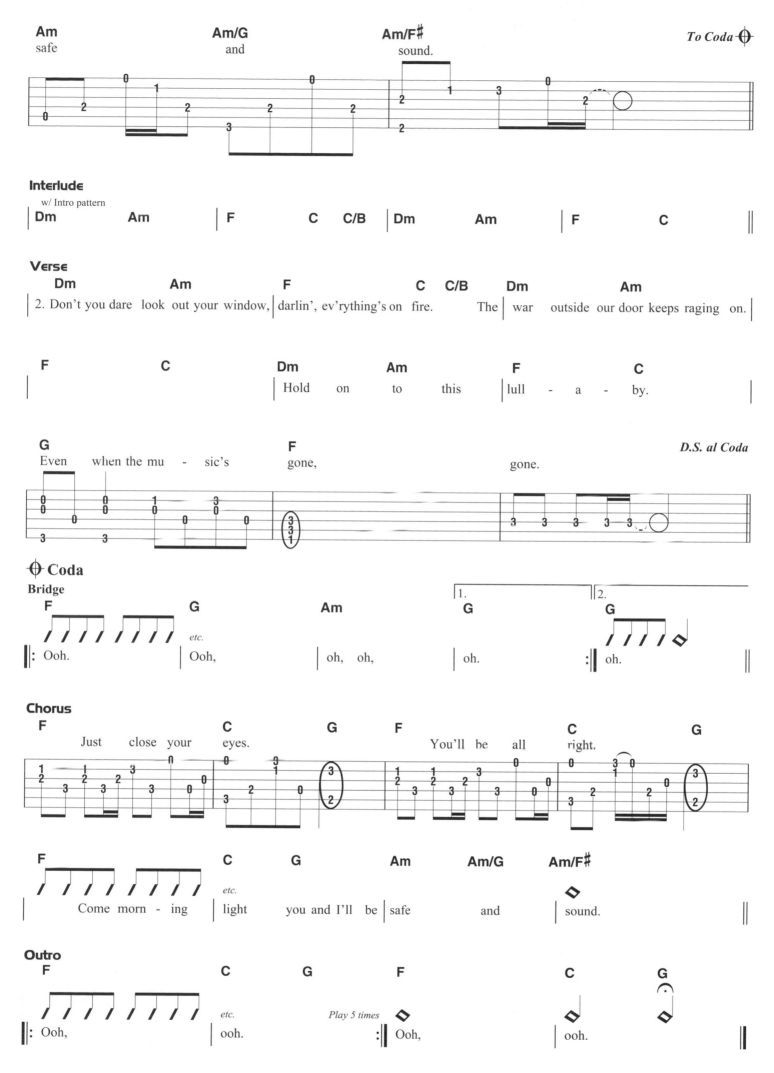

Say It Ain't So

Words and Music by Rivers Cuomo

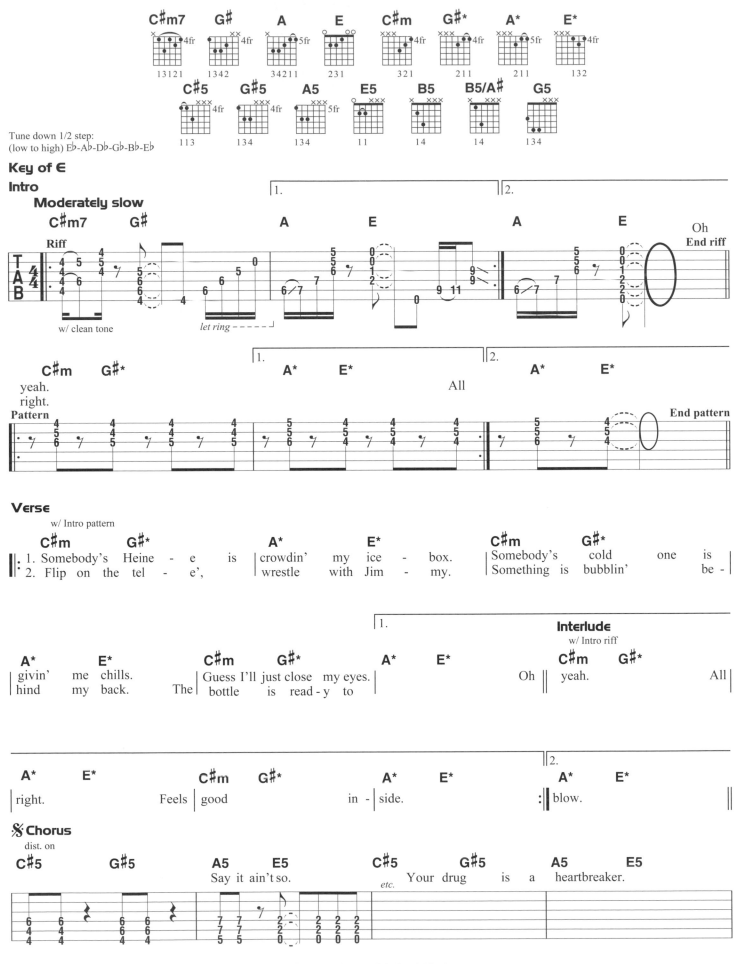

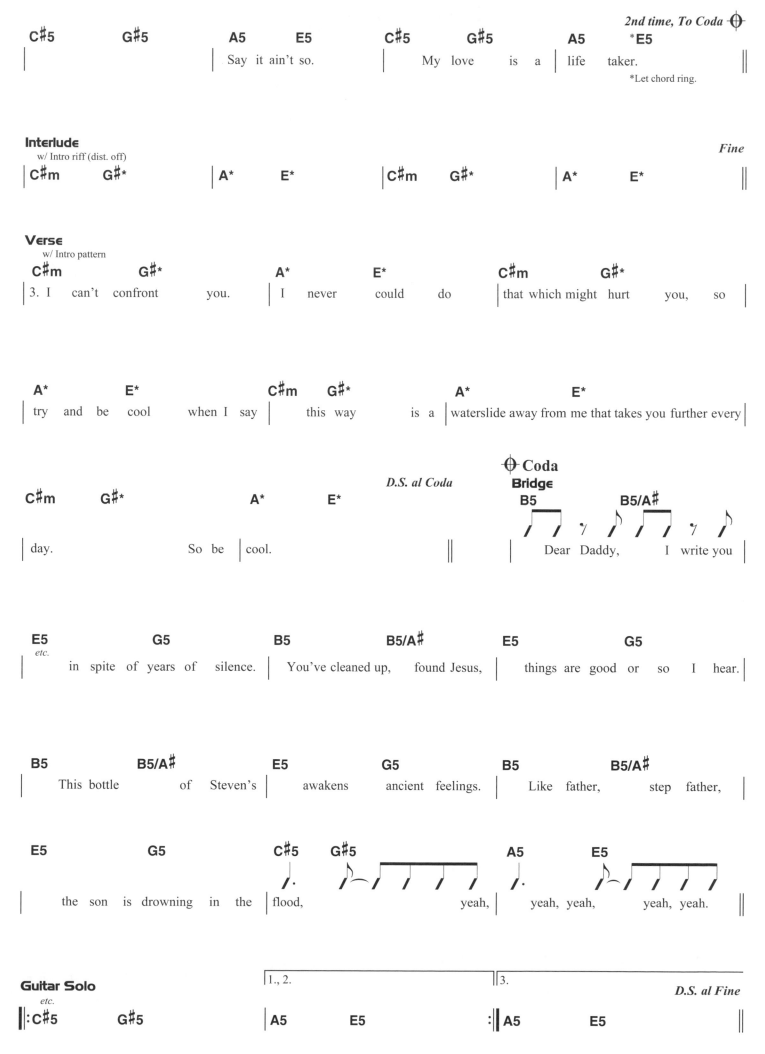

Scar Tissue

Words and Music by Anthony Kiedis, Flea, John Frusciante and Chad Smith

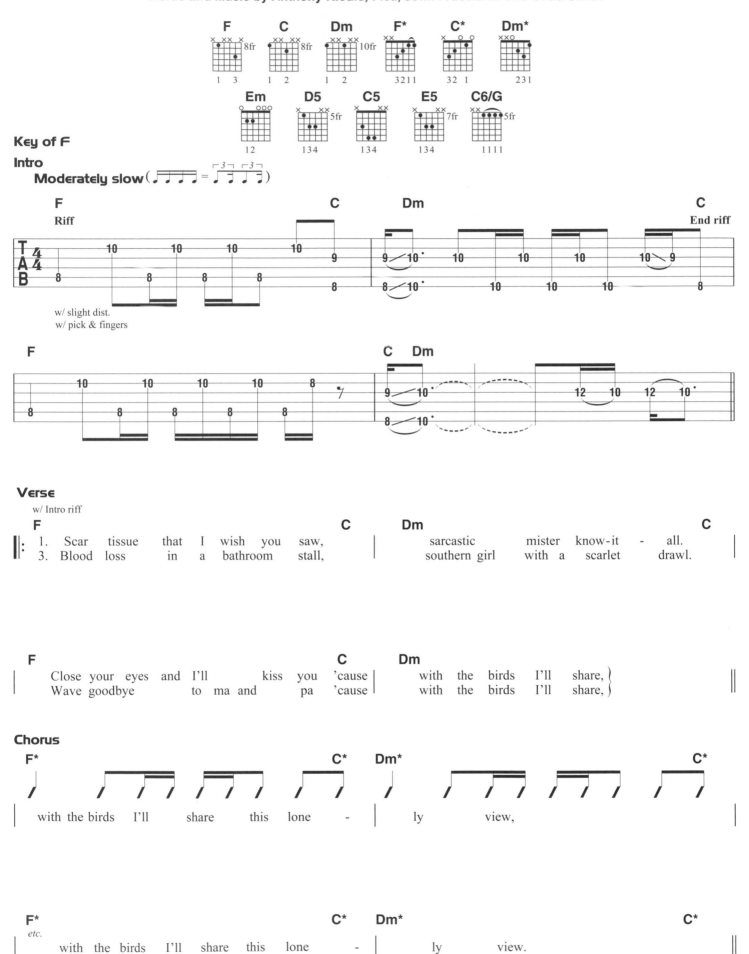

𝄌 Verse

w/ Intro riff

| F | | C | Dm | | C |

2. Push me up against the wall, | young Kentucky girl in a push up bra.
4. Soft spoken with a broken jaw, | step outside but not to brawl.
5. *See additional lyrics*

| F | | C | Dm | | |

Fallin' all over myself to lick | your heart and taste your health 'cause
Autumn's sweet, we call it fall, I'll | make it to the moon if I have to crawl, and

Chorus

w/ Chorus pattern

| F* | | C* | Dm* | | C* |

with the birds I'll share this lone - | ly view,

| F* | | C* | Dm* | | C* |

with the birds I'll share this lone - | ly view,

To Coda ⊕

| F* | | C* | Dm* | | |

with the birds I'll share this lone - | ly view.

1.

Guitar Solo

| Dm* | | | C* | Dm* | Em :‖

2.

Guitar Solo

| D5 | | | C5 | D5 | |

D.S. al Coda

| | | | C5 | D5 | E5 ‖

⊕ Coda

Outro-Guitar Solo

1., 2. **4.**

| Dm* | | | C6/G | Dm* ‖ C6/G | Dm* |

grad. slower

‖: | | C6/G | Dm* :‖ | 𝄐 ‖

Additional Lyrics

5. Scar tissue that I wish you saw,
Sarcastic mister know-it-all.
Ah, close your eyes and I'll kiss you 'cause
With the birds I'll share…

Semi-Charmed Life

Words and Music by Stephan Jenkins

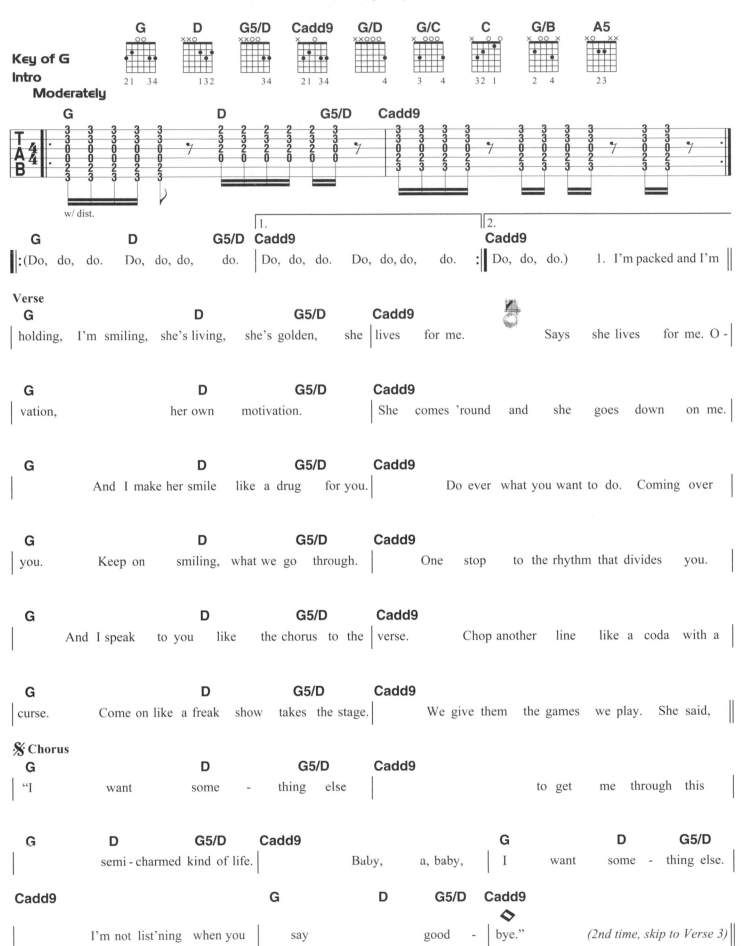

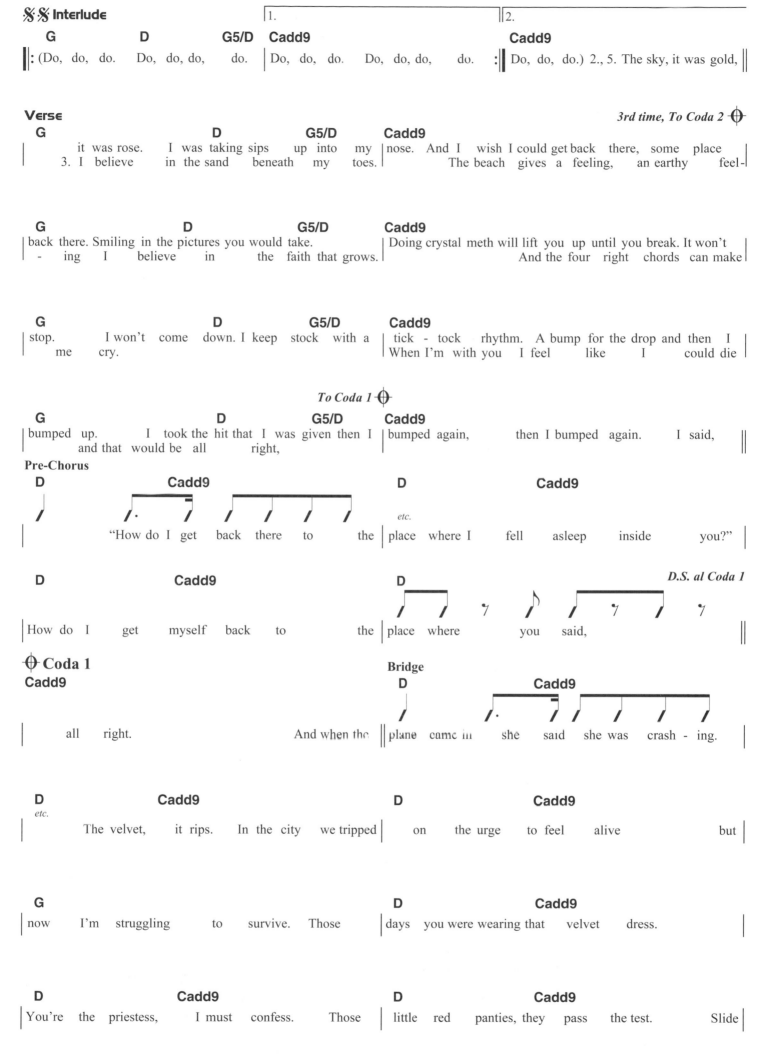

G	N.C.			G/D	G/C	

up around the belly face down on the mattress. | One. | And you |

G/D	G/C		G/D	G/C		G

hold me, and we are | broken. | Still, it's | all that I want to do, just a little, now. ‖

Verse

w/ Intro pattern

G	D	G5/D	Cadd9			

4. Feel myself, head made of the ground. | I'm scared, I'm not coming down, |

G	D	G5/D	Cadd9		G	D	G5/D

no, no. | And I won't run for my | life. |

Cadd9		G	D	G5/D	Cadd9	

She's got her jaws now locked down in a smile | but nothing is all right, | all right. And ‖

Chorus

pick chords

G	D	C		G	D	

I want something else | to get me | through this |

C		G	D	C	

life. Baby, | I want something else. | Not list'ning |

G	D		C	G/B	A5	

when you say good - bye, good -

Play 3 times

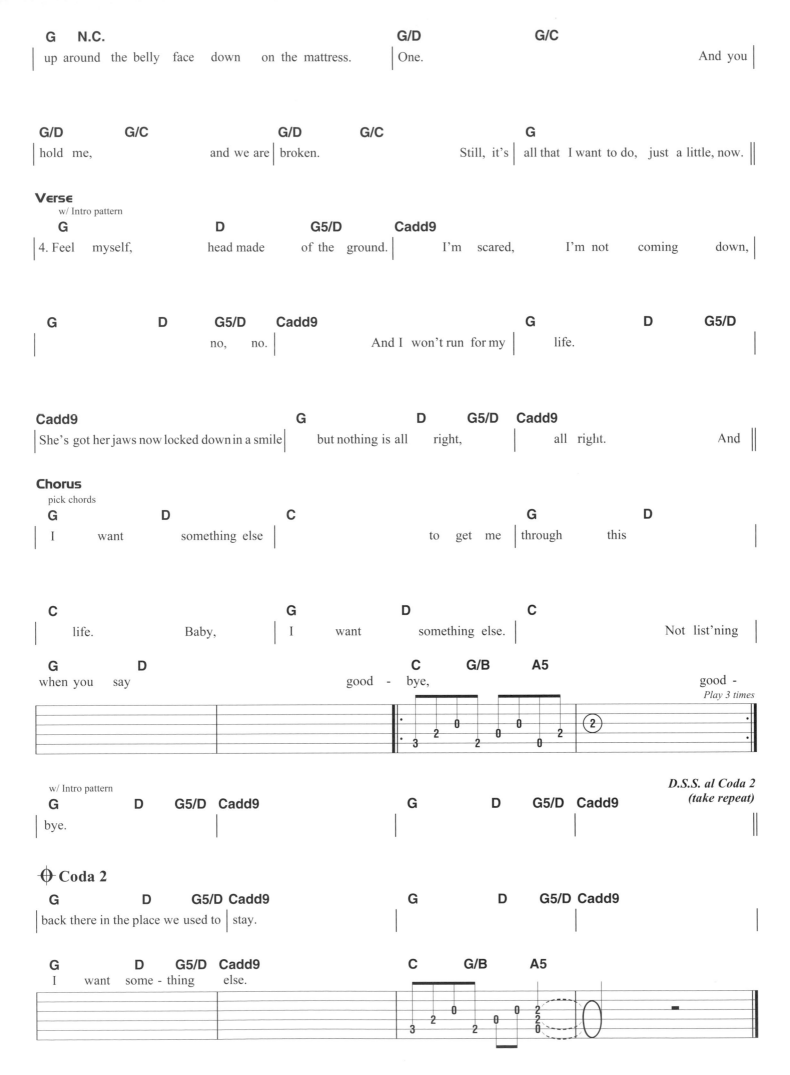

w/ Intro pattern

G	D	G5/D	Cadd9		G	D	G5/D	Cadd9

bye. ‖

D.S.S. al Coda 2
(take repeat)

Coda 2

G	D	G5/D	Cadd9		G	D	G5/D	Cadd9

back there in the place we used to | stay. |

G	D	G5/D	Cadd9		C	G/B	A5

I want some - thing else.

This Land Is Your Land

Words and Music by Woody Guthrie

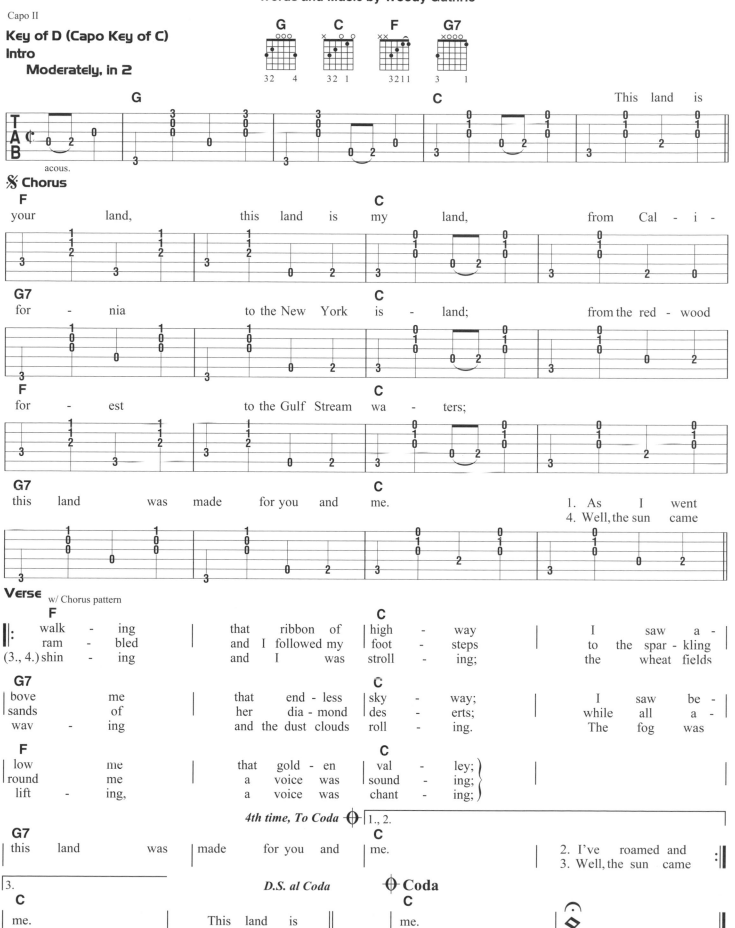

Simple Man

Words and Music by Ronnie Van Zant and Gary Rossington

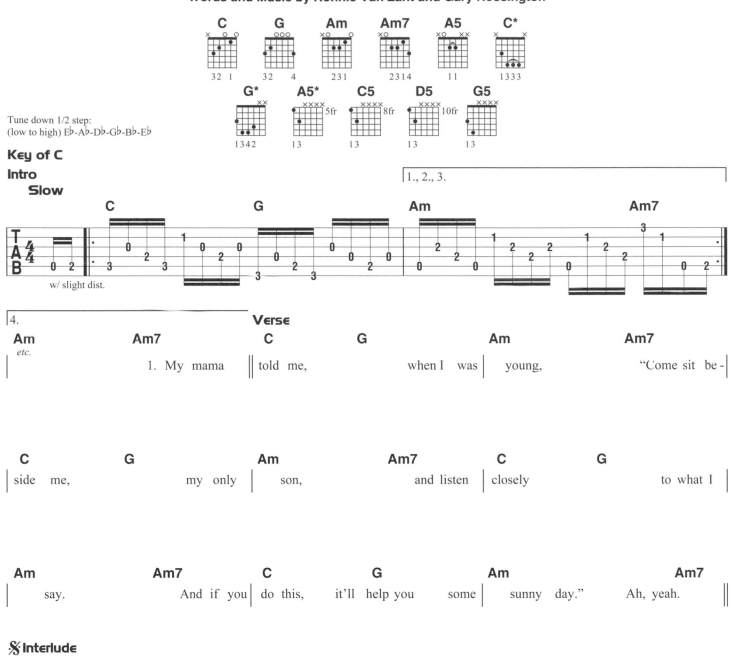

Tune down 1/2 step:
(low to high) E♭-A♭-D♭-G♭-B♭-E♭

Key of C

Intro

Slow

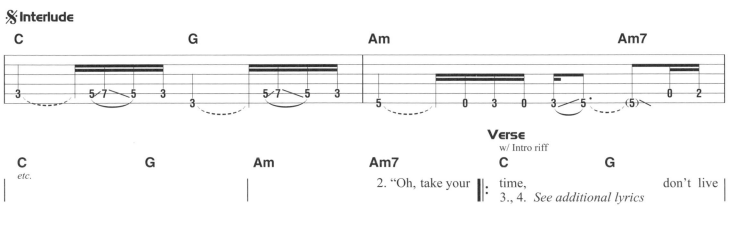

Am etc.

1. My mama | told me,   when I was | young,   "Come sit be-

C   G   Am   Am7   C   G

| side me,   my only | son,   and listen | closely   to what I |

Am   Am7   C   G   Am   Am7

| say.   And if you | do this,   it'll help you   some | sunny day."   Ah, yeah. ‖

% Interlude

C   G   Am   Am7

C etc.   G   Am   Am7   C   G

Verse
w/ Intro riff

2. "Oh, take your | time,   don't live
3., 4. *See additional lyrics*

Am   Am7   C   G   Am   Am7

| too fast.   Troubles will | come,   and they will | pass.   Go find a |

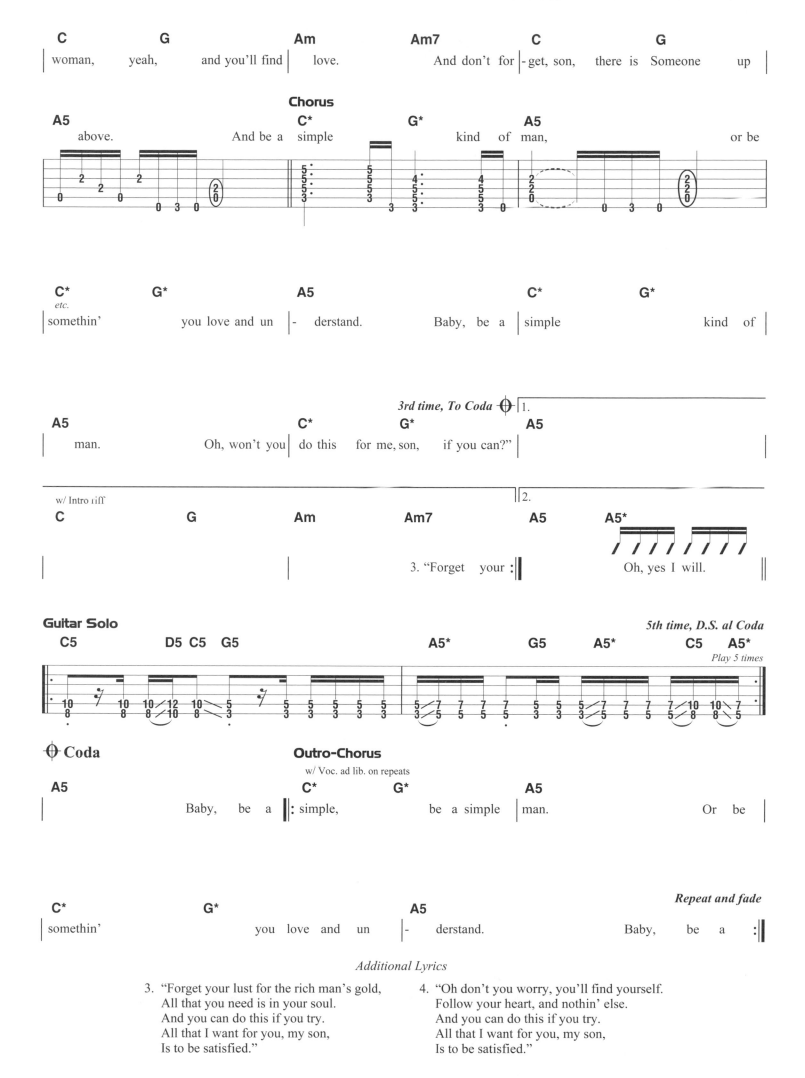

Space Oddity

Words and Music by David Bowie

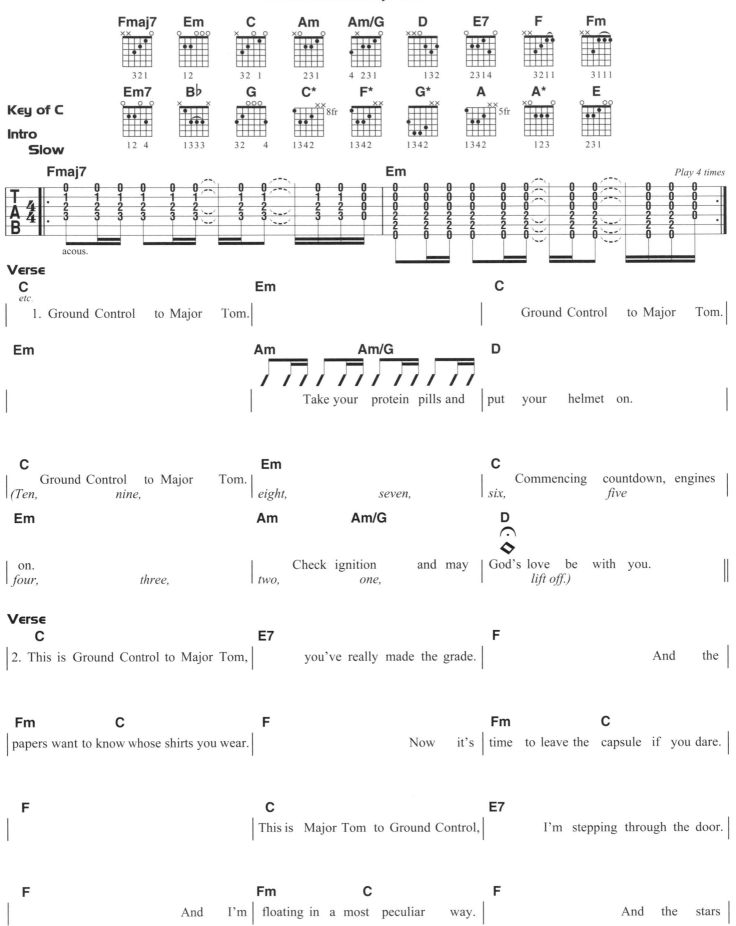

Key of C
Intro
Slow

Verse

C   Em   C
etc.
1. Ground Control to Major Tom. | Ground Control to Major Tom.

Em   Am   Am/G   D

Take your protein pills and | put your helmet on.

C   Em   C
Ground Control to Major Tom. | Commencing countdown, engines
(Ten,   nine, | eight,   seven, | six,   *five*

Em   Am   Am/G   D
on. | Check ignition and may | God's love be with you.
four,   *three,* | *two,*   *one,* | *lift off.)*

Verse

C   E7   F
2. This is Ground Control to Major Tom, | you've really made the grade. | And the

Fm   C   F   Fm   C
papers want to know whose shirts you wear. | Now it's | time to leave the capsule if you dare.

F   C   E7
| This is Major Tom to Ground Control, | I'm stepping through the door.

F   Fm   C   F
And I'm | floating in a most peculiar way. | And the stars

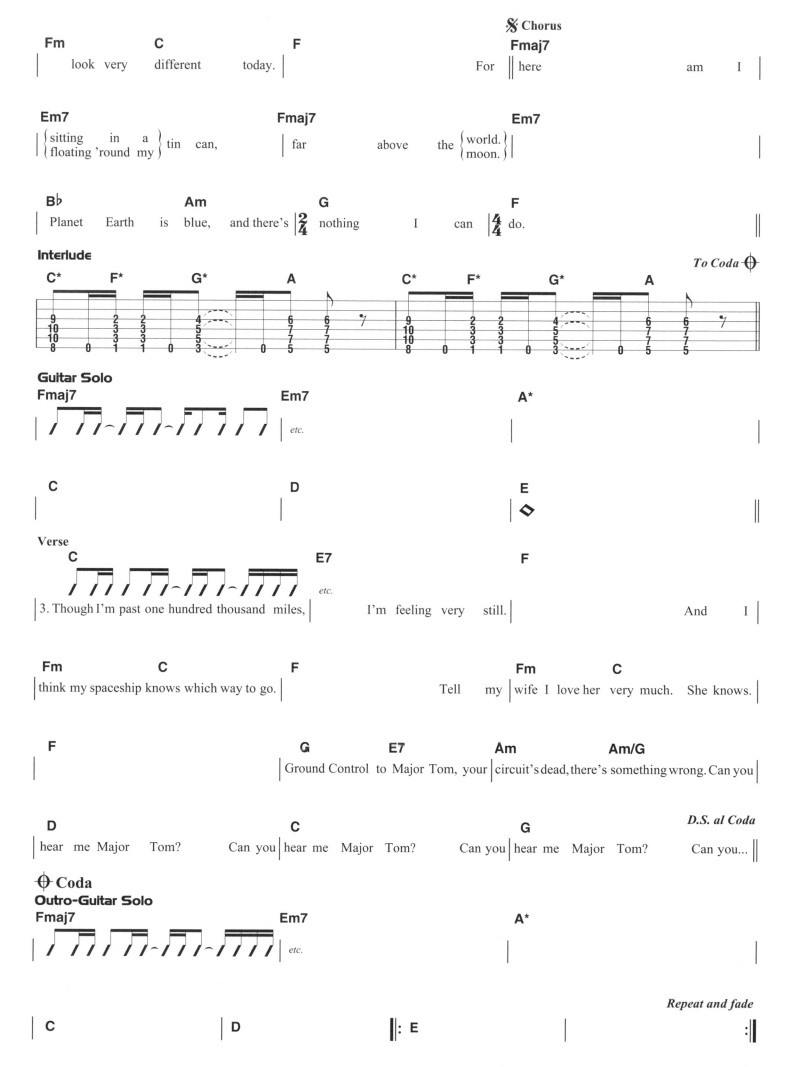

Story of My Life

Words and Music by Jamie Scott, John Henry Ryan, Julian Bunetta,
Harry Styles, Liam Payne, Louis Tomlinson, Niall Horan and Zain Malik

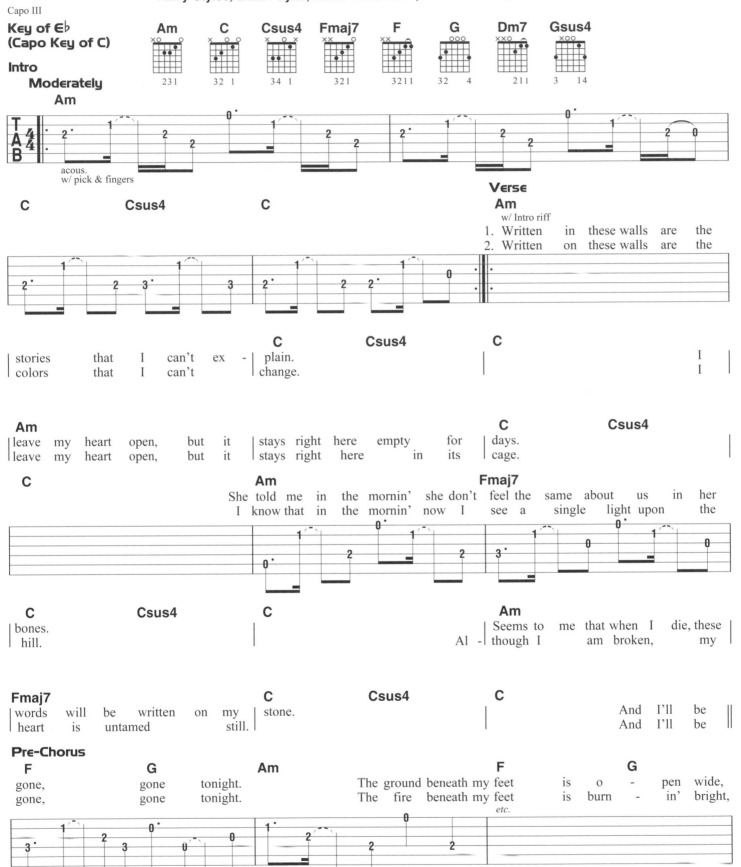

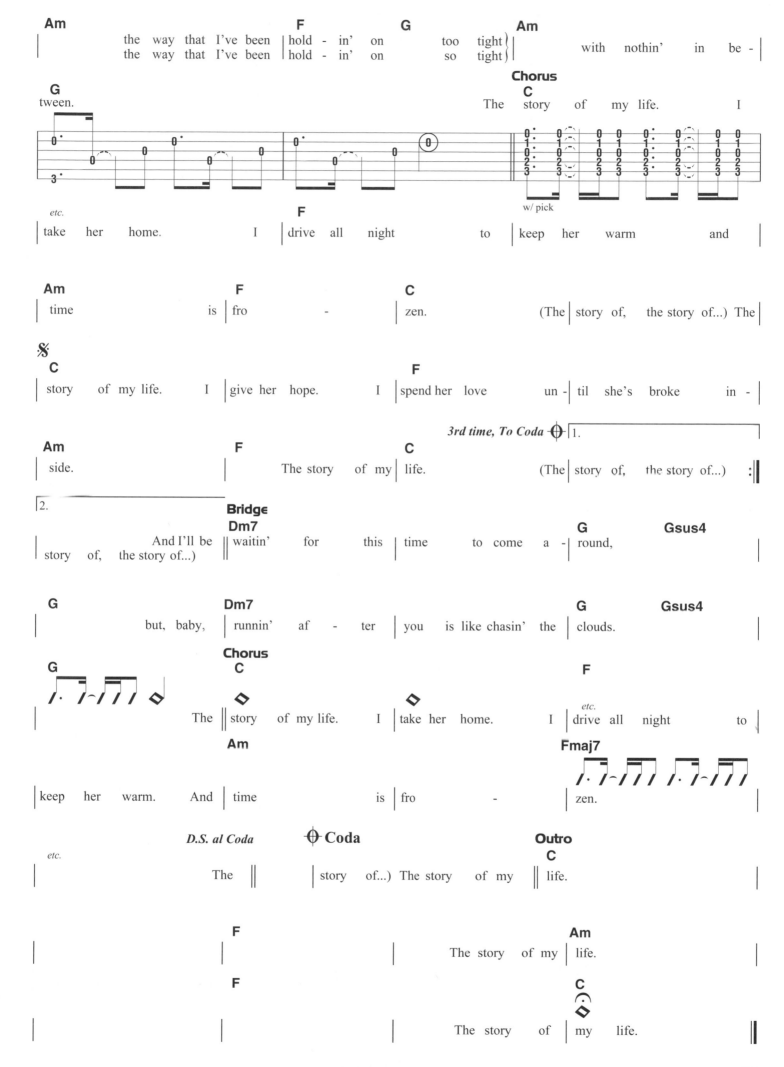

Tears in Heaven

Words and Music by Eric Clapton and Will Jennings

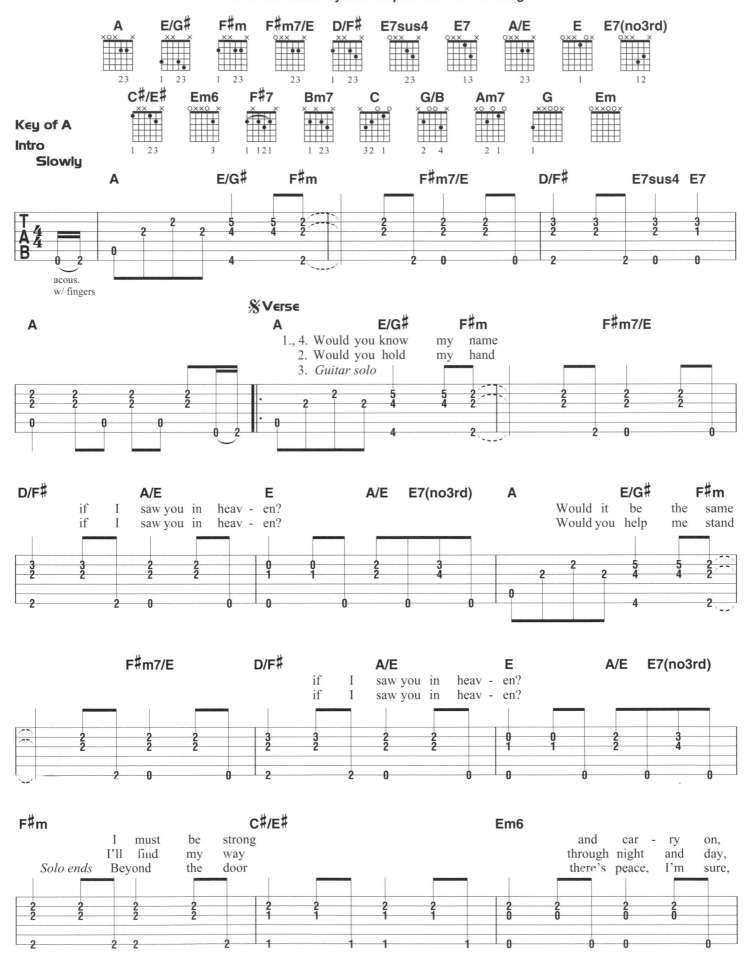

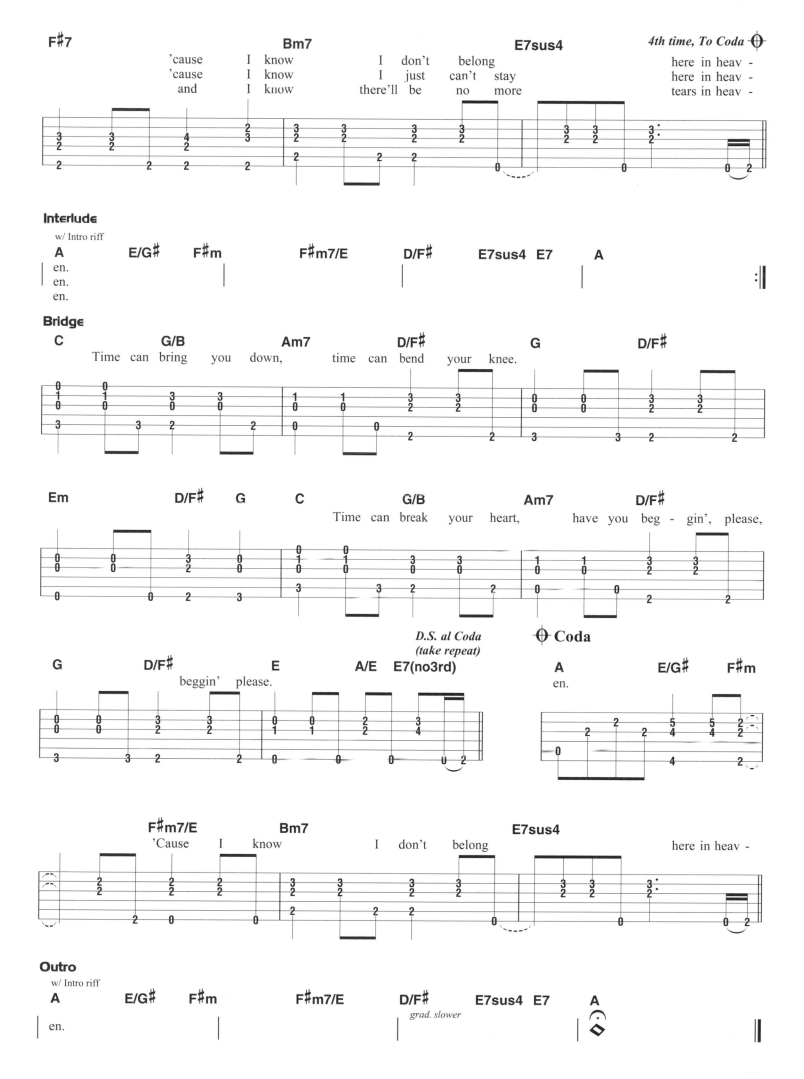

Tube Snake Boogie

Words and Music by Billy F Gibbons, Dusty Hill and Frank Beard

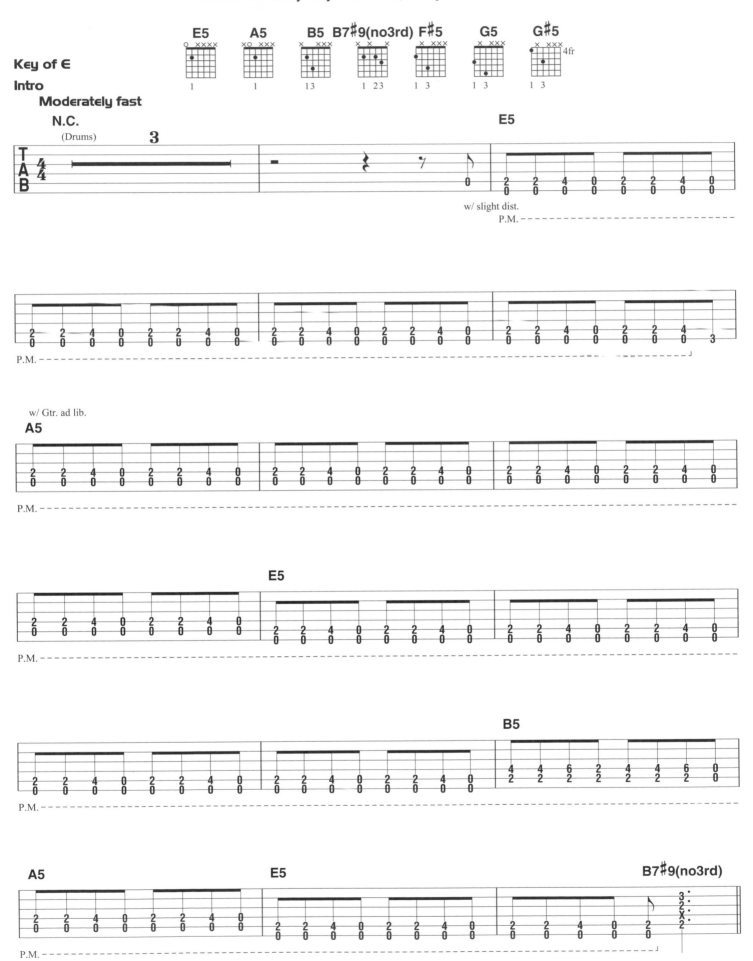

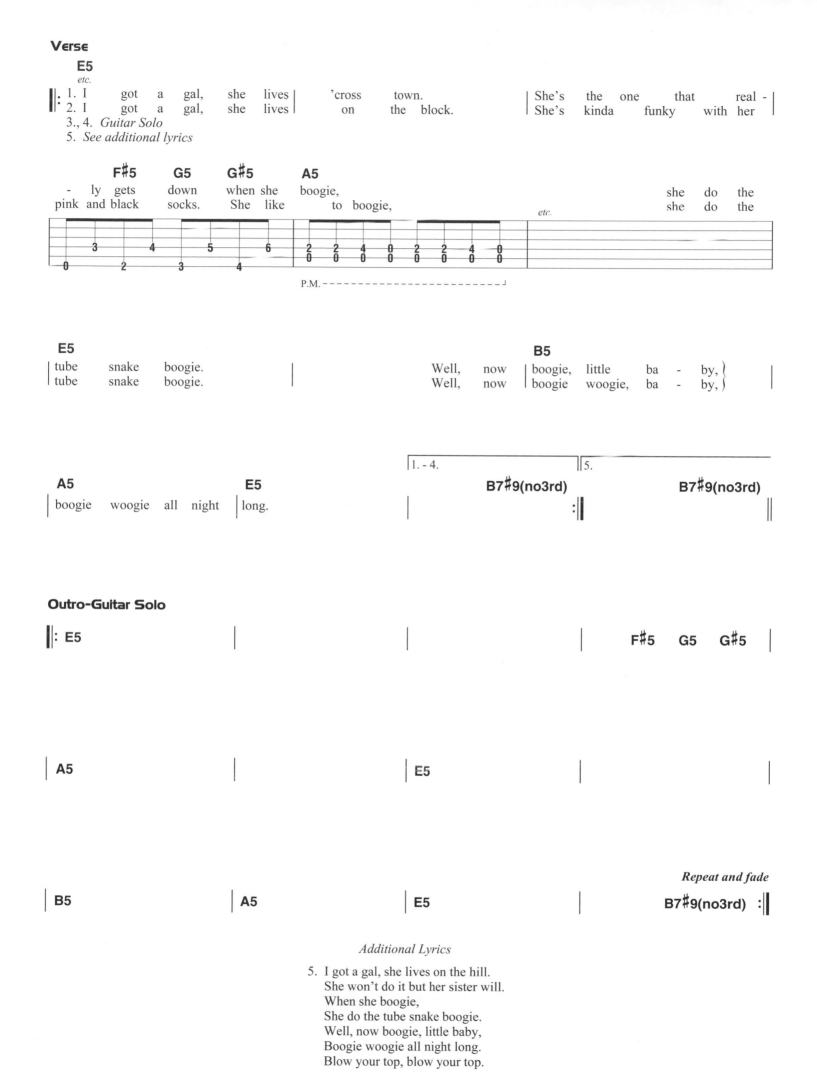

Waiting on the World to Change

Words and Music by John Mayer

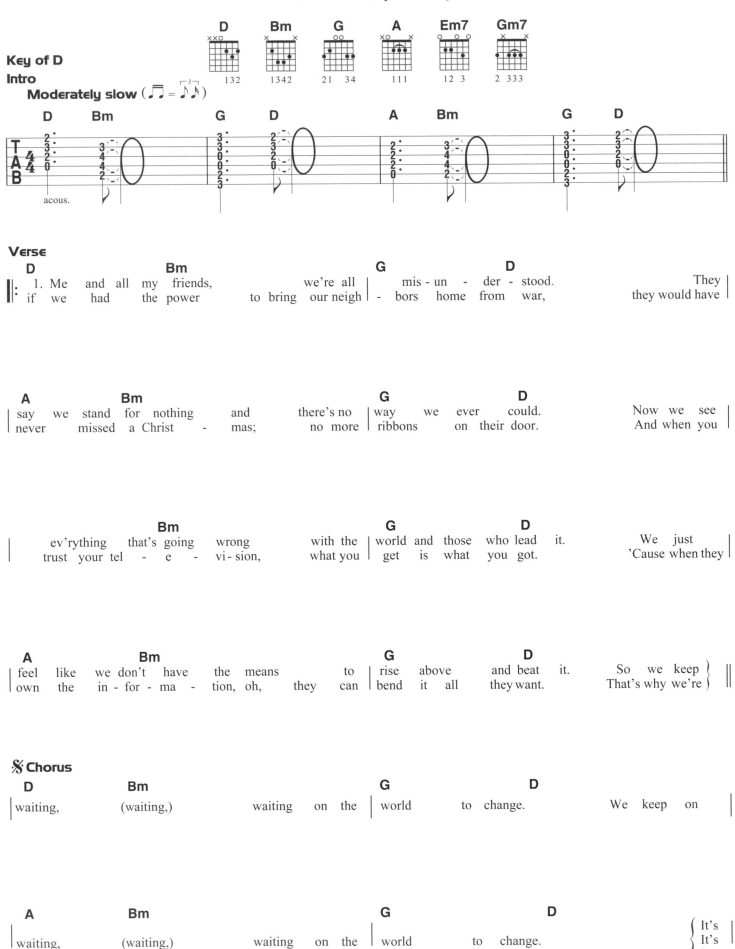

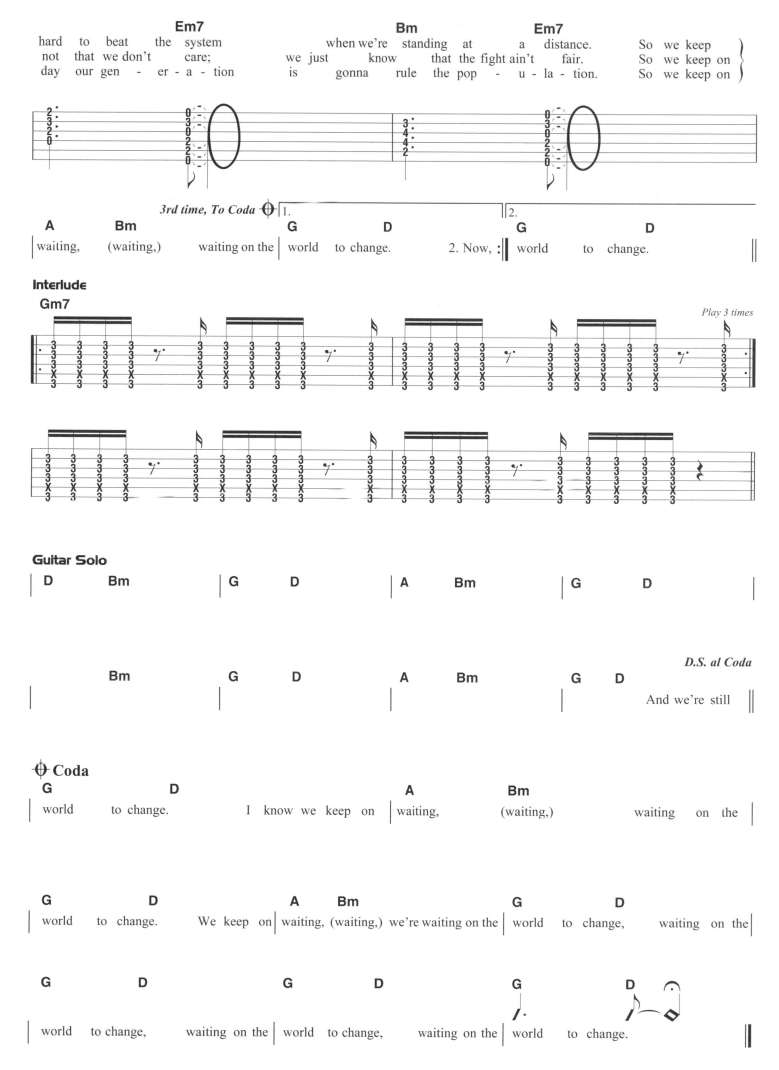

Em7

hard to beat the system ... when we're standing at a distance. So we keep
not that we don't care; ... we just know that the fight ain't fair. So we keep on
day our gen - er - a - tion ... is gonna rule the pop - u - la - tion. So we keep on

Bm   **Em7**

3rd time, To Coda ⊕ 1.

A   Bm   **G   D**   **G   D**

| waiting, (waiting,) waiting on the | world to change. 2. Now, : || world to change. ||

Interlude

Gm7

Play 3 times

Guitar Solo

| D   Bm | G   D | A   Bm | G   D |

D.S. al Coda

| Bm | G   D | A   Bm | G   D |
And we're still ||

⊕ **Coda**

G   D   A   Bm

| world to change. I know we keep on | waiting, (waiting,) waiting on the |

G   D   A   Bm   G   D

| world to change. We keep on | waiting, (waiting,) we're waiting on the | world to change, waiting on the |

G   D   G   D   G   D

| world to change, waiting on the | world to change, waiting on the | world to change. ||

Wake Me Up When September Ends

Words by Billie Joe
Music by Green Day

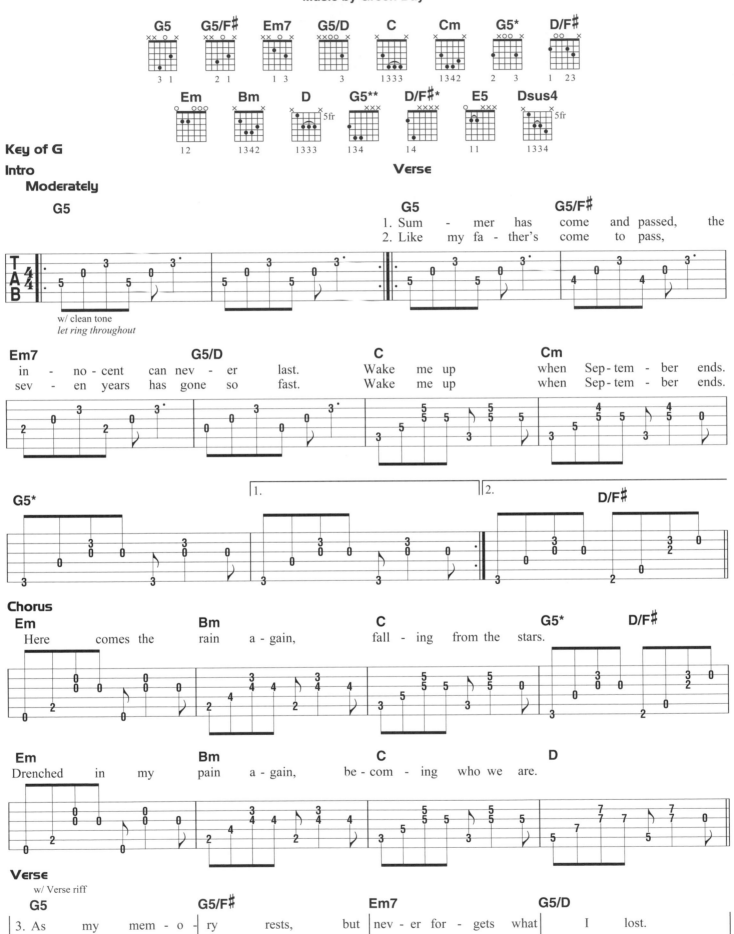

Key of G

Intro
Moderately

Verse

1. Sum - mer has come and passed, the
2. Like my fa - ther's come to pass,

in - no - cent can nev - er last. Wake me up when Sep - tem - ber ends.
sev - en years has gone so fast. Wake me up when Sep - tem - ber ends.

Chorus

Here comes the rain a - gain, fall - ing from the stars.

Drenched in my pain a - gain, be - com - ing who we are.

Verse
w/ Verse riff

3. As my mem - o - ry rests, but nev - er for - gets what I lost.

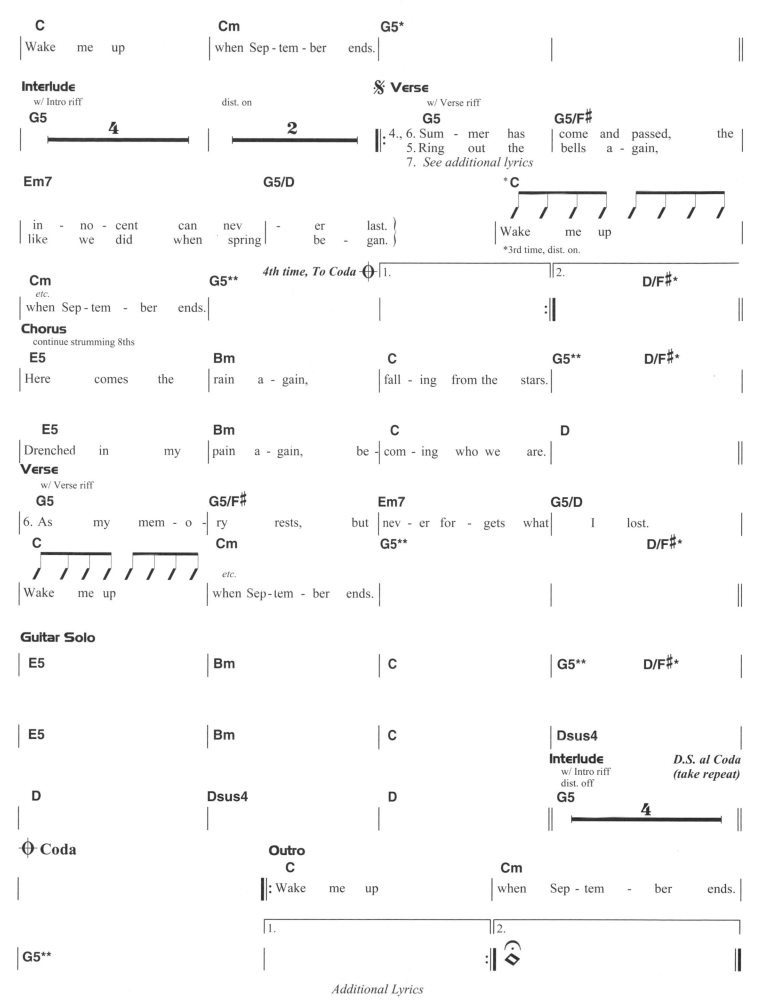

Walk Don't Run

By Johnny Smith

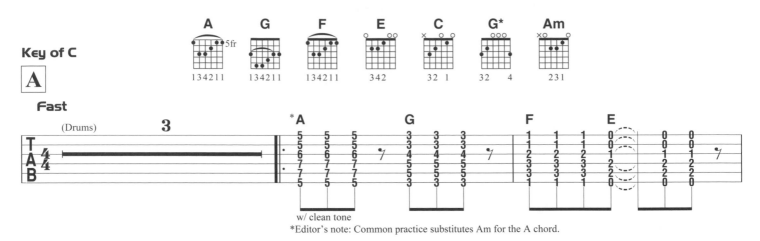

Key of C

A

Fast

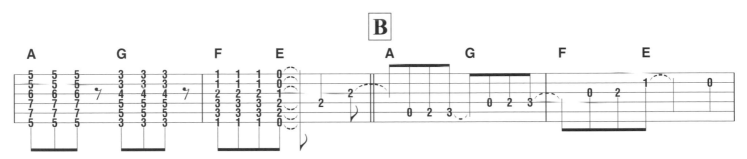

w/ clean tone

*Editor's note: Common practice substitutes Am for the A chord.

B

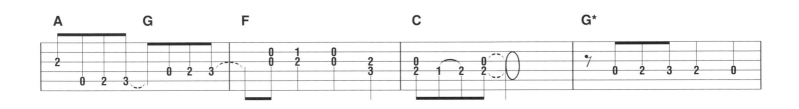

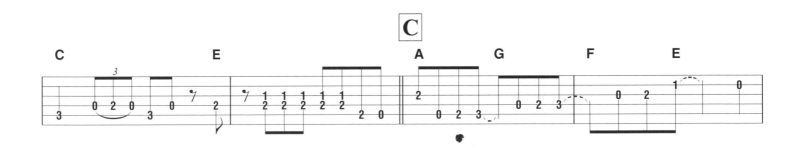

C

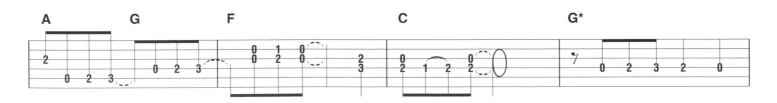

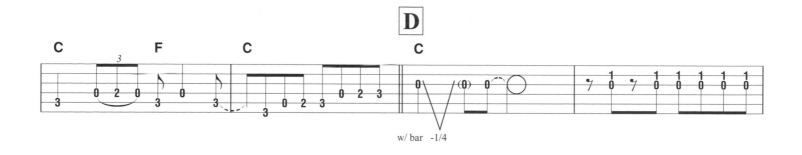

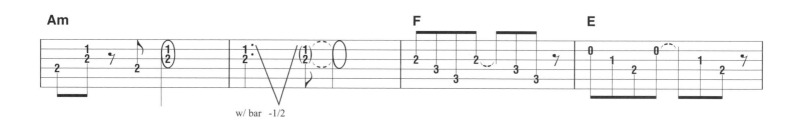

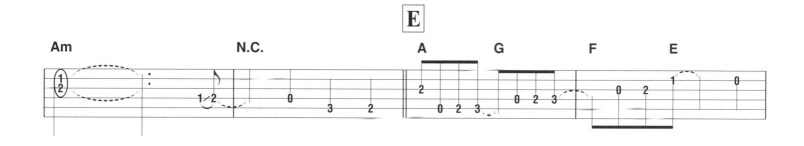

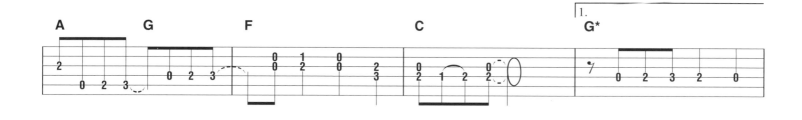

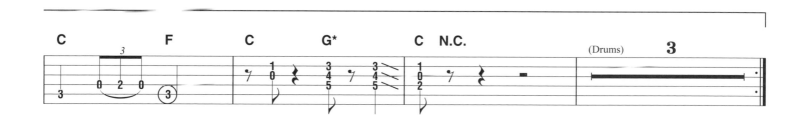

With or Without You

Words and Music by U2

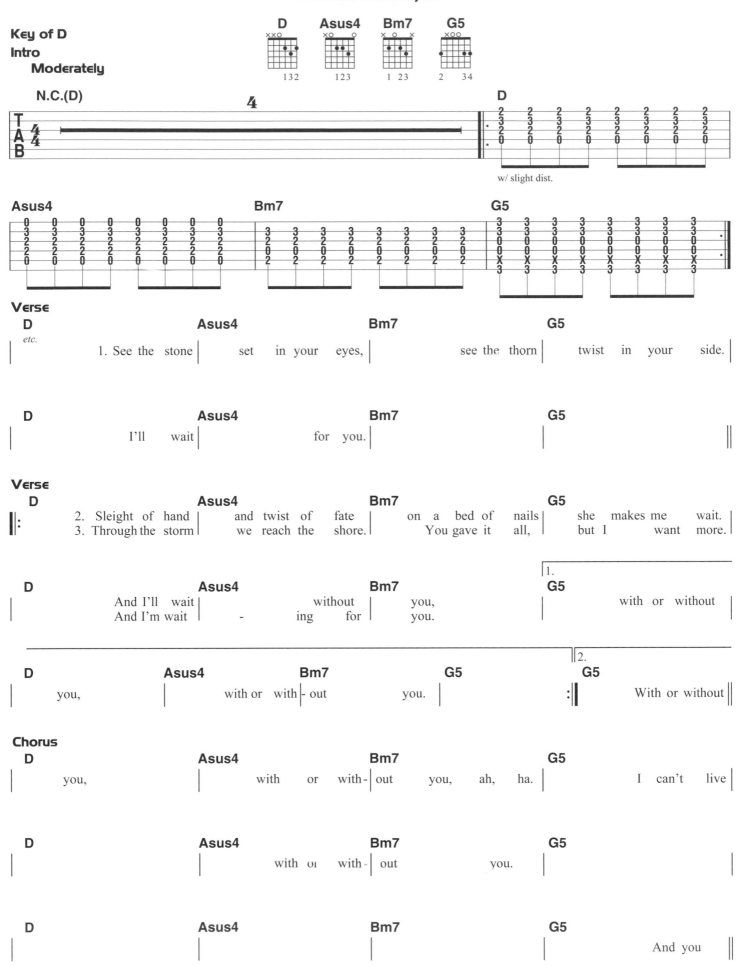

Yesterday

Words and Music by John Lennon and Paul McCartney

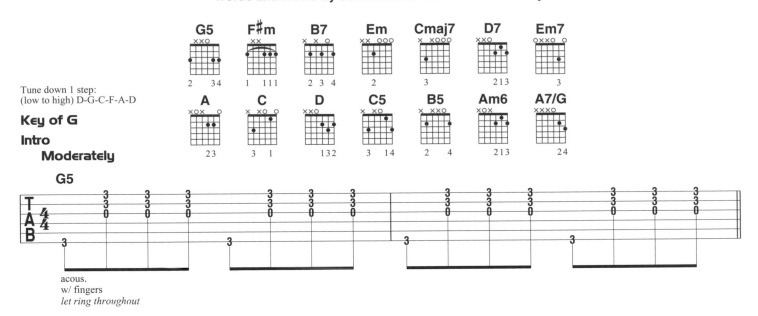

Tune down 1 step:
(low to high) D-G-C-F-A-D

Key of G

Intro

Moderately

acous.
w/ fingers
let ring throughout

Verse

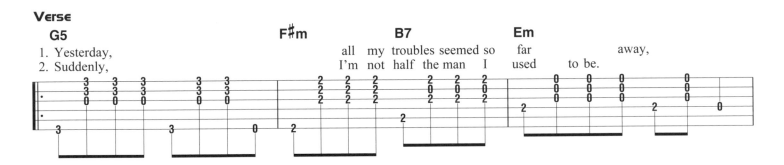

1. Yesterday,
2. Suddenly,

all my troubles seemed so far away,
I'm not half the man I used to be.

now it looks as though they're here to stay.
There's a shadow hanging o - ver me.

Oh, I believe in
Oh, believe yesterday

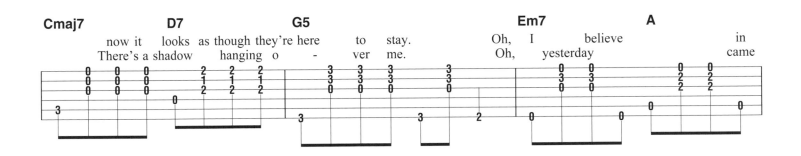

Bridge

yes - ter - day.
sud - den - ly.

Why she had to go, I don't

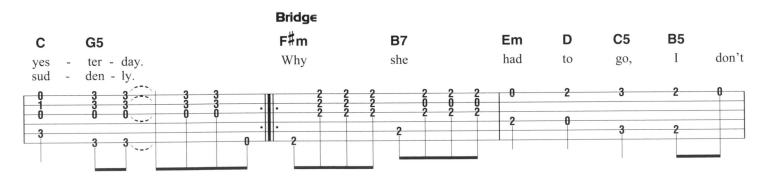

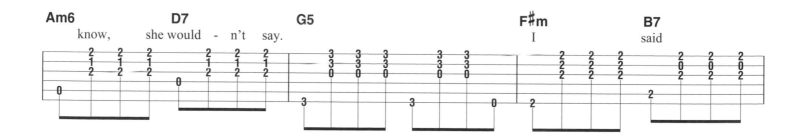

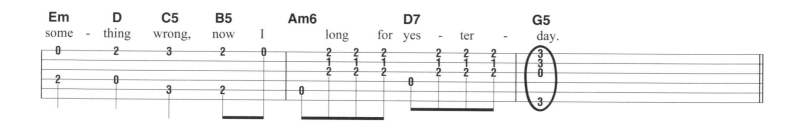

Verse

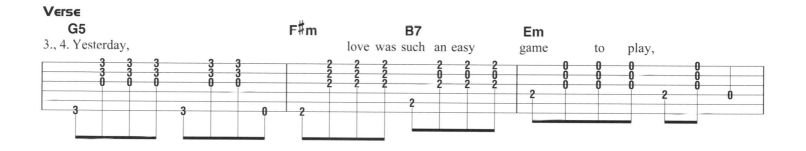

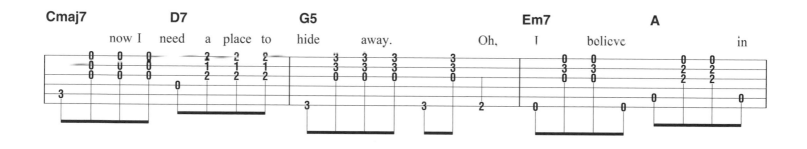

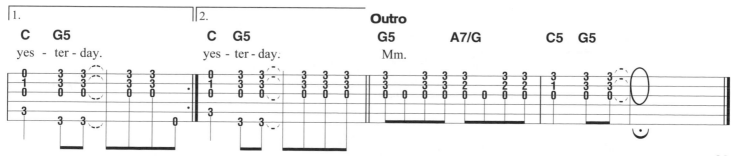

Zombie

Lyrics and Music by Dolores O'Riordan

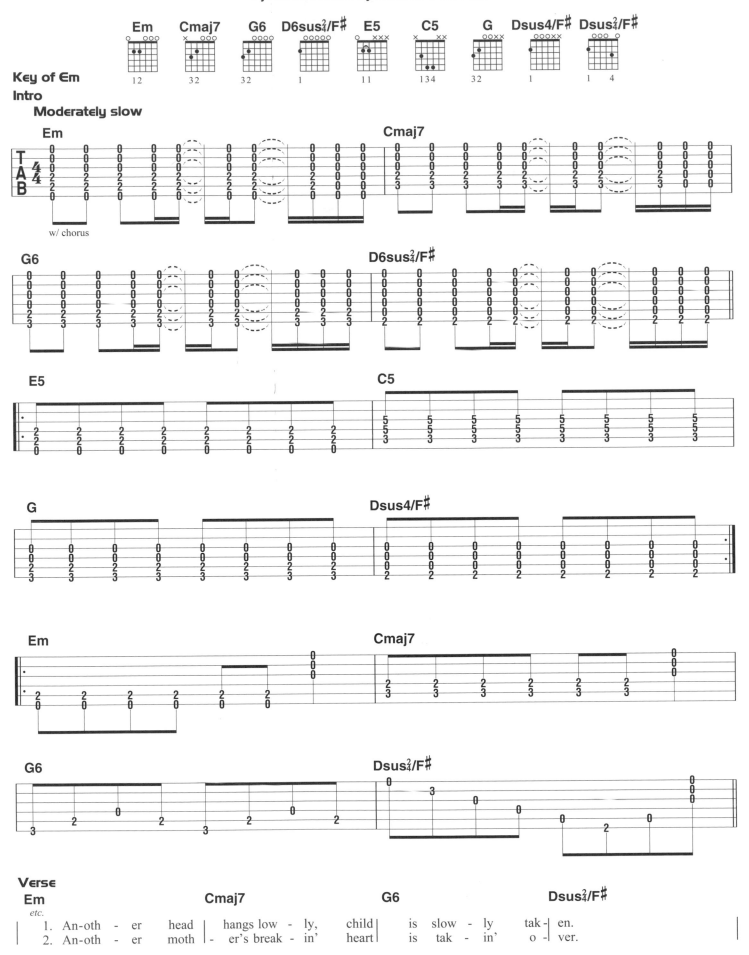

Key of Em

Intro

Moderately slow

1. An-oth - er head hangs low - ly, child is slow - ly tak - en.
2. An-oth - er moth - er's break - in' heart is tak - in' o - ver.

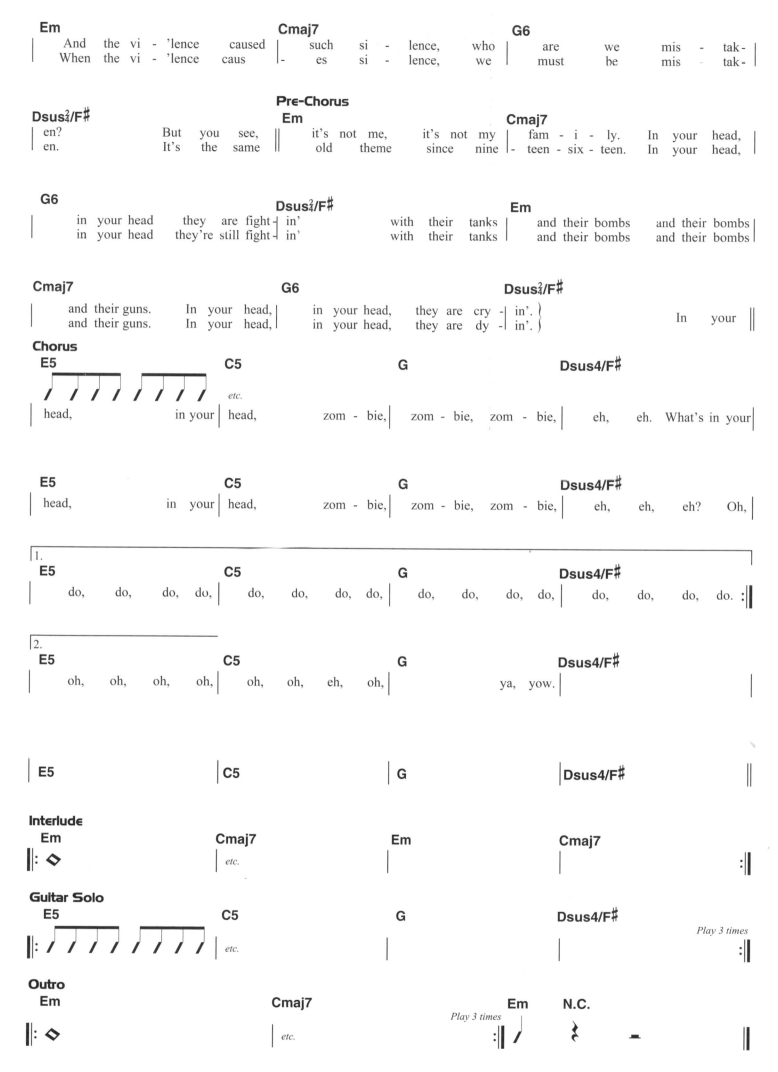

RHYTHM TAB LEGEND

Rhythm Tab is a form of notation that adds rhythmic values to the traditional tab staff.

TABLATURE graphically represents the guitar fingerboard. Each horizontal line represents a string, and each number represents a fret. Rhythmic values are shown using ovals, stems, and dots.

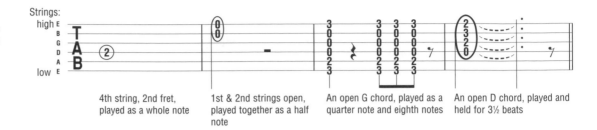

4th string, 2nd fret, played as a whole note

1st & 2nd strings open, played together as a half note

An open G chord, played as a quarter note and eighth notes

An open D chord, played and held for 3½ beats

Definitions for Special Guitar Notation

HALF-STEP BEND: Strike the note and bend up 1/2 step.

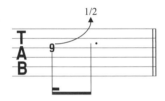

WHOLE-STEP BEND: Strike the note and bend up one step.

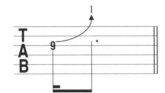

SLIGHT (MICROTONE) BEND: Strike the note and bend up 1/4 step.

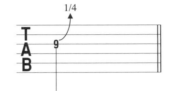

BEND AND RELEASE: Strike the note and bend up as indicated, then release back to the original note. Only the first note is struck.

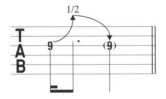

PRE-BEND: Bend the note as indicated, then strike it.

GRACE NOTE PRE-BEND AND RELEASE: Bend the note as indicated. Strike it and release the bend back to the original note.

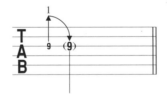

UNISON BEND: Strike the two notes simultaneously and bend the lower note up to the pitch of the higher.

HOLD BEND: While sustaining bent note, strike note on different string.

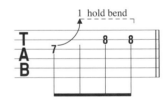

VIBRATO: The string is vibrated by rapidly bending and releasing the note with the fretting hand.

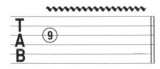

WIDE VIBRATO: The pitch is varied to a greater degree by vibrating with the fretting hand.

HAMMER-ON: Strike the first (lower) note with one finger, then sound the higher note (on the same string) with another finger by fretting it without picking.

PULL-OFF: Place both fingers on the notes to be sounded. Strike the first note and without picking, pull the finger off to sound the second (lower) note.

HAMMER FROM NOWHERE: Sound note(s) by hammering with fret hand finger only.

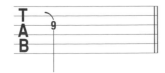

GRACE NOTE SLUR: Strike the note and immediately hammer-on (or pull-off) as indicated.

GRACE NOTE SLUR (CLUSTER): Strike the notes and immediately hammer-on (or pull-off) as indicated.

LEGATO SLIDE: Strike the first note and then slide the same fret-hand finger up or down to the second note. The second note is not struck.

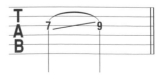

SHIFT SLIDE: Same as legato slide, except the second note is struck.

GRACE NOTE SLIDE: Quickly slide into the note from below or above.

TRILL: Very rapidly alternate between the notes indicated by continuously hammering on and pulling off.

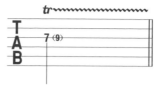

TAPPING: Hammer ("tap") the fret indicated with the pick-hand index or middle finger and pull off to the note fretted by the fret hand.

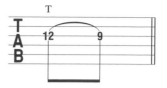

NATURAL HARMONIC: Strike the note while the fret-hand lightly touches the string directly over the fret indicated.

Harm.

PINCH HARMONIC: The note is fretted normally and a harmonic is produced by adding the edge of the thumb or the tip of the index finger of the pick hand to the normal pick attack.

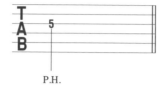

P.H.

HARP HARMONIC: The note is fretted normally and a harmonic is produced by gently resting the pick hand's index finger directly above the indicated fret (in parentheses) while the pick hand's thumb or pick assists by plucking the appropriate string.

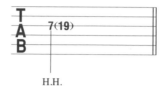

H.H.

PICK SCRAPE: The edge of the pick is rubbed down (or up) the string, producing a scratchy sound.

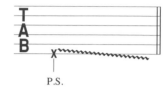

P.S.

MUFFLED STRINGS: A percussive sound is produced by laying the fret hand across the string(s) without depressing, and striking them with the pick hand.

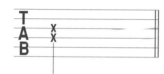

PALM MUTING: The note is partially muted by the pick hand lightly touching the string(s) just before the bridge.

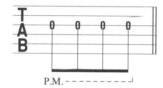

P.M. - - - - - - - - - ⌐

RAKE: Drag the pick across the strings indicated with a single motion.

rake - ⌐

TREMOLO PICKING: The note is picked as rapidly and continuously as possible.

ARPEGGIATE: Play the notes of the chord indicated by quickly rolling them from bottom to top.

VIBRATO BAR DIVE AND RETURN: The pitch of the note or chord is dropped a specified number of steps (in rhythm), then returned to the original pitch.

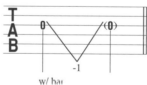

w/ bar

VIBRATO BAR SCOOP: Depress the bar just before striking the note, then quickly release the bar.

w/ bar - - - - - - - ⌐

VIBRATO BAR DIP: Strike the note and then immediately drop a specified number of steps, then release back to the original pitch.

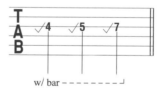

w/ bar - - - - - - ⌐

Additional Musical Definitions

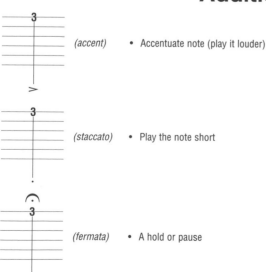

(accent) • Accentuate note (play it louder)

(staccato) • Play the note short

(fermata) • A hold or pause

⊓ • Downstroke

V • Upstroke

• Repeat measures between signs

NOTE: Tablature numbers in parentheses are used when:
• The note is sustained, but a new articulation begins (such as a hammer-on, pull-off, slide, or bend), or
• A bend is released.
• A note sustains while crossing from one staff to another.